TELL-TALE MURDER

A Play in Three Acts

by

PHILIP WEATHERS

SAMUEL FRENCH

LONDON
NEW YORK   TORONTO   SYDNEY   HOLLYWOOD

Copyright © 1956 by Philip Weathers
All Rights Reserved

TELL-TALE MURDER is fully protected under the copyright laws of the British Commonwealth, including Canada, the United States of America, and all other countries of the Copyright Union. All rights, including professional and amateur stage productions, recitation, lecturing, public reading, motion picture, radio broadcasting, television and the rights of translation into foreign languages are strictly reserved.

ISBN 978-0-573-01439-0
www.samuelfrench.co.uk
www.samuelfrench.com

FOR AMATEUR PRODUCTION ENQUIRIES

UNITED KINGDOM AND WORLD
EXCLUDING NORTH AMERICA
plays@samuelfrench.co.uk
020 7255 4302/01

Each title is subject to availability from Samuel French, depending upon country of performance.

CAUTION: Professional and amateur producers are hereby warned that *TELL-TALE MURDER* is subject to a licensing fee. Publication of this play does not imply availability for performance. Both amateurs and professionals considering a production are strongly advised to apply to the appropriate agent before starting rehearsals, advertising, or booking a theatre. A licensing fee must be paid whether the title is presented for charity or gain and whether or not admission is charged.

The Professional Rights in this play are controlled by Eric Glass Ltd, 25 Ladbroke Cres, Notting Hill, London W11 1PS.

No one shall make any changes in this title for the purpose of production. No part of this book may be reproduced, stored in a retrieval system, or transmitted in any form, by any means, now known or yet to be invented, including mechanical, electronic, photocopying, recording, videotaping, or otherwise, without the prior written permission of the publisher. No one shall upload this title, or part of this title, to any social media websites.

The right of Philip Weathers to be identified as author of this work has been asserted in accordance with Section 77 of the Copyright, Designs and Patents Act 1988.

TELL-TALE MURDER

Presented by Linnit and Dunfee Ltd at the Grand Theatre, Blackpool, on the 22nd December 1952, with the following cast of characters:

JANE MANNION 50	*Freda Jackson*
BENTLEY RICHMOND 60	*D. A. Clarke-Smith*
ELLEN OLD 80ish	*Susan Richards*
DAVID MANNION 26	*Joss Ackland*
MAUREEN RICHMOND 24	*Heather Stannard*
VANESSA MANNION	*Janet Reid*
RICHARD MANNION	*Richard Caldicott*
HOWELL	*Thomas Heathcote*

SYNOPSIS OF SCENES

The action of the play passes in the living-room of "Porthenis", Jane Mannion's house on the Cornish coast

ACT I
SCENE 1 An evening in September
SCENE 2 After supper, the same evening

ACT II
The following evening about 9 o'clock

ACT III
SCENE 1 Midday, the following day
SCENE 2 Evening, the following Friday

Time—the present

PRODUCTION NOTES

The casting of "Jane Mannion" presents difficulties, but providing she is the right actress, a woman between thirty and forty is probably most suitable for the part. For the first flash-back she can under-dress to a certain extent, and the removal of her grey wig and the reddening of her lips should be sufficient to give the impression that though young, she is tired and harassed. For the second flash-back she has considerably more time to make the more important changes of make-up. But a quick-change room is necessary either on the rostrum of the staircase, or near to it.

Howell's difficult change, and that only because of time, is after the second flash-back, when he will need help in putting on his chauffeur's jacket. If necessary he can be speaking his lines as he does this. If he wants to grey his hair, and providing his colouring is fairish, the powder will not show in the second flash-back, owing to the dimness of the lighting.

In order not to reveal too much too soon, it is preferable that the cast list on the programme should not be in order of appearance, nor should it state relationships.

ACT I

Scene 1

Scene—*The living-room of "Porthenis", Jane Mannion's house on the Cornish coast. An evening in September.*

The room is Elizabethan. It has a most definite personality, but no charm, and no "lived-in" quality. At night, with the lamps throwing pools of light, and the corners shadowy, it has a foreboding atmosphere. Across the corner up L, *an oriel window forms a large bay, the centre portion consisting of french windows leading to the garden, with a view of the moor, the cliff edge and the sea beyond. A door down* L *leads to other parts of the house. A staircase,* R.C *of the back wall, runs up and off* R. *There is a large cupboard built in under the stairs. The staircase is of carved black oak, its walls fully panelled to match; the bluish-grey stone walls of the rest of the room have a deep, more plainly carved dado of the same wood. The floor is of large flagstones. The furniture is mainly Elizabethan. The wall* R *has a recess in which stands a dresser. There are two circular tables, four carved oak armchairs, a pouffe, and a chest high enough to be used as a table. A grandfather clock and a large gong on a stand are above and below the window respectively. A wall mirror hangs above the gong. At night, the room is lit by oil-lamps, one on the chest, one on the table up* L.C. *and one on the table* C.

(*See the Ground Plan at the end of the play*)

When the Curtain *rises,* Jane Mannion *is sitting* C, *sewing. The oil-lamp on the table* C *is fully turned up, but the other lamps though lit, are very low, so that Jane is in a pool of light. The windows, and the window curtains are open, and the upstage part of the room is lit and coloured by a fine sunset.* Jane *is a Cornishwoman, somewhere around fifty years old, a fine, upstanding woman, still handsome, but her face, though scarcely lined, has something closed and secretive about it, and her manner is in keeping with her face. She is aloof, apparently completely self-controlled, and poised, and speaks without a trace of Cornish accent. She is used to complete command in her very small world. Her dresses, though not necessarily old-fashioned, are made so that they almost touch the ground, and she wears sombre colours. Her iron-grey hair is well-dressed, with a heavy plait over her head from ear to ear, which tends to increase her height. For a time she continues intent on her fine sewing, then she hears the buzzing of a bluebottle flying about the room. She looks up, annoyed, and with an occasional quick movement of the head, follows the bluebottle's flight. When it gets nearer to her a strained look comes to her face as slowly it settles on the large rug in the centre of the stage. She watches it, fascinated, as apparently it crawls across the rug from* L *to* R. *Her hand slowly goes out to the fly swatter on the table* C *and closes on the handle. Before she can lift it, the bluebottle buzzes off the floor on to the table* C. *Carefully she lifts the swatter, holds it poised for a moment, then swiftly swats and kills the insect, the noise sharply breaking the tense silence. She puts down the swatter and her sewing, rises, picks up the bluebottle, moves swiftly to the french windows and throws it out.* ELLEN, *the housekeeper, enters down* L, *carrying a tray with four sherry glasses. She crosses towards the chest.* ELLEN *is small and very old, nearly eighty. Her face is brown and heavily wrinkled, her knitted eyebrows overhang her black, beady eyes, so that she has to peer upwards to see who she is talking to, but her hair has not turned white. Except when she is alone with* Jane, *she is watchful and guarded, another secretive Cornishwoman. Although she is physically active for her age, her mind lapses at times into senility, she inclines to chuckle in a mirthless way, and mutter between her toothless jaws. She has a Cornish accent.*

JANE. Flies again.
ELLEN (*pausing* LC; *with a low chuckle*) You'll never get rid of 'em—not now.
JANE. I hate them.

(ELLEN *moves towards the chest*)

(*She moves to Ellen*) Let me look at those glasses.
ELLEN (*grumblingly*) They're clean enough.
JANE (*picking up the glasses and looking at them in the light of the lamp*) You've been getting careless lately.

(ELLEN *grunts*)

Did you put clean towels in the bedroom?
ELLEN. Yes.
JANE. And the soap?
ELLEN (*impatiently*) Yes, yes.
JANE (*indicating the glasses*) They're all right. (*She picks up a book from the table* C *and puts it in the cupboard*)
ELLEN (*putting the tray on the chest*) Of course they are, I've got a new polishing cloth at last.
JANE. Is the chauffeur's bed aired?
ELLEN. Chauffeur's! It's bad enough to have a visitor, without him bringing a chauffeur. (*She turns to go*)
JANE. Is the bed aired?
ELLEN (*pausing up* C) No—no, I forgot.
JANE. Then do it now.
ELLEN (*turning to the stairs*) Fuss, fuss, fuss.
JANE. And, Ellen.

(ELLEN *pauses on the first stair*)

(*She moves to* R *of Ellen*) I don't want you about when this man

Bentley Richmond comes. You must be ill. Keep to your room.

ELLEN (*coming off the stair; rebelliously*) Why should I? I like to know what's doing. You always push me out of the way when strangers come.

JANE. Your memory's going.

ELLEN. I remember years ago well enough. (*Plaintively*) It's "now" I forget.

JANE. And you say silly things.

ELLEN (*looking evilly at her*) Some people I know'd be interested to hear 'em.

JANE (*with a hint of blackmail*) Bentley Richmond's a lawyer, Ellen.

(ELLEN *almost spits in her dislike of lawyers*)

So when you've seen to that bed, get to your room and stay there.

(ELLEN, *muttering, starts up the stairs*)

(*She moves below the table* C, *picks up her sewing and faces Ellen*) It's time David was down.

ELLEN. I'll tell him.

JANE. He forgets everything when he's busy writing.

ELLEN. He hasn't done much writing *this* day. (*She goes up the stairs*)

(DAVID MANNION *enters quickly down the stairs, almost banging into Ellen. He is a tall, good-looking young man of twenty-six, dark, but in other ways completely unlike his mother. He has been to a public school and a university, and follows his father's profession as a novelist*)

(*To David*) Oh, there you are.

(ELLEN, *muttering, exits up the stairs*)

DAVID (*pausing and looking after Ellen*) Really, you know—(*he moves* LC) Ellen's getting worse every day. Why don't you . . . ?

JANE. Get rid of her?

DAVID. No, no. But pension her off.

JANE (*sitting in the chair* C) Ellen's been a good servant to me, David. While she wants to stay, she can stay.

DAVID. Well, I suppose I can always put her in my next novel, but it'll have to be a "whodunnit".

JANE (*reproachfully*) David!

DAVID (*embarrassed*) Oh, sorry, Mother. (*He moves to the windows*) I can't think what's happened to Maureen. She *should* have been here an hour ago.

JANE (*sewing*) D'you expect doctors to be punctual? Especially lady doctors.

DAVID (*moving down* LC) But dammit all, this is a special occasion. Her old man'll be here any minute. I'm nervous enough about meeting him as it is—if she's not here it'll be hell.

JANE. I don't see why.

DAVID (*crossing to* RC) Well, you know how it is—want to make a good impression, and all that. Rather wish you hadn't asked him to stay here now. The pub in the village isn't bad.

JANE. I wanted him to get to know us.

DAVID. You're a queer woman. I'll never understand you.

JANE. Won't you, David?

DAVID. You've shown pretty plainly you don't want me to marry Maureen, yet here you are, doing all you can to entertain her father.

JANE. You tell me he's a famous man in his own country. I haven't known any famous men.

DAVID. If you *will* shut yourself up here for years, you can't expect to.

JANE. What else *could* I do?

DAVID. You could have packed up and gone ages ago.

JANE. Run away?

DAVID. But how can you *stand* it here?

JANE. I've learnt to.

DAVID (*moving above the chair* RC) Well, I haven't. The life we're living here's impossible. All this suspicion—this—this *ostracism*—I tell you it's getting on my nerves. Wherever I go—mutter, mutter, mutter—whisper, whisper, whisper. It's—it's . . .

JANE (*her voice hard*) It's Cornwall.

DAVID. And that's precisely why I'm off to South Africa.

JANE. But why do you have to go to *South Africa?*

DAVID (*moving to* R *of the table* C) Because I must think of the *future*. My capital's limited——

JANE. Then . . .

DAVID. —my books don't bring in much, and my influence here in England's *nil*. Out there, there's an opening for a publisher . . .

JANE. But you're not a publisher.

DAVID. It's what I want to be. I'll have to start in a small way, of course, but Bentley Richmond can pull strings—get the right people interested in me.

JANE. Can't he do that here?

DAVID. Not to the same extent. And in any case, Maureen wants to go.

JANE. Ah!

DAVID. Well, it's natural, isn't it? Wanting to be near her father?

JANE. And you *don't* want to be near your mother.

DAVID (*moving above the chair* RC) There's no need to put it like that.

JANE. Isn't there?

DAVID. I just don't intend to stay in this house—or in Cornwall.

JANE. And I do.

DAVID (*moving down* RC) But it isn't a practical proposition (*More reasonably*) Look, Mother, I've been going through some figures upstairs. (*He takes a sheet of paper from his pocket and sits in the chair* RC) Mr Richmond's bound to ask me about my financial position, and I've worked it out. In addition to five thousand pounds to cover my education, father left about fifteen thousand pounds in securities, and this house, didn't he?

JANE. Yes.

DAVID. He left you the use of it all . . .

JANE (*bitterly*) Providing I didn't marry again.

DAVID. Yes—until *I* married. Then I come into three-quarters of it, and you have the remaining quarter.

JANE (*stopping sewing*) How can I live on that? It's ridiculous!

DAVID. Then surely you must see *why* we must sell this house.

JANE. I won't sell.

DAVID. But . . .

JANE. Don't you understand, David? It's my home. I've lived here for nearly thirty years.

DAVID. We've got to face facts.

JANE. But that's just what you're *not* doing. You'll never sell this house, because no-one'll buy it. (*She resumes sewing*) It's too big—too far away from anywhere—it needs thousands of pounds to put it in repair. It simply isn't *worth* anything.

DAVID (*rising*) Well, we'll soon find *that* out. (*He moves up* R) I'll put a surveyor in.

JANE (*after a short pause*) A surveyor!

DAVID (*indicating the walls up* R) He can test all the fabric—(*he looks at the ceiling*) look at the roof—and . . . (*he looks at the floor*)

JANE (*interrupting*) No, David.

DAVID (*moving above the table* C) Why not?

JANE. Until you marry, this house is mine, David, and I won't have strangers in it. You know that already.

DAVID (*moving* LC) What you mean is you won't do anything to help sell it.

JANE. No, I won't. When you've turned me out . . .

DAVID. I'm not turning you out.

JANE. What are you doing then?

DAVID (*moving down* LC) I'm trying to make you see reason.

JANE. Don't my wishes mean anything to you?

DAVID. Of course they do.

JANE. Then why don't you let me live on here, even after you're married.

DAVID. Because it'd be better if you got away.

JANE. No.

DAVID. Better for Vanessa, too. This is no place for her to live. Take her where she'll meet girls of her own age—somewhere she can be trained to earn her own living.

JANE. I don't want her to earn her living. I want to stay here, and I want her to stay with me.

(*Off stage the front door bell jangles rustily*)

DAVID. That'll be Bentley Richmond. We'll have to talk about this later.
JANE. I've nothing more to say.
DAVID. But . . .
JANE. Hadn't you better let the great man in?

(DAVID *looks at* JANE *a moment then exits down* L. JANE *betrays slight nervous apprehension, rises, moves to the lamp up* RC, *turns it up, then moves above the table* C. *She pauses at the sound of David's voice, and listens forebodingly to the offstage conversation*)

DAVID (*off*) It's too bad of Maureen, but it must be something important that's kept her.
BENTLEY (*off*) Well, I've waited a year—another hour or so won't make much difference.
DAVID (*off*) Let me take your coat.
BENTLEY (*off*) Thank you.

(JANE *picks up the lamp from the table* C *and puts it on the dresser* R)

DAVID (*off*) Come and meet mother.

(JANE *moves below the table* C.
BENTLEY RICHMOND *enters down* L *followed by* DAVID.
Bentley is a fine-looking man of about sixty, extremely intelligent, with a sensitive face and clear-cut features; eyes which can be kindly or piercing; a musical, well-modulated voice and an almost Edwardian courtesy of manner. He is dressed in a dark double-breasted suit which has been made to suit his personality as well as his figure, and he wears a stock. He crosses to JANE, *who without moving from her position, holds out her hand to him.* DAVID *closes the door*)

JANE (*gracious in an Edwardian way*) Welcome to "Porthenis", Mr Richmond.
BENTLEY (*holding her hand in both his without shaking it*) Thank you, ma'am. It's a pleasure I've looked forward to for some time.

(DAVID *crosses to the chest and pours three glasses of sherry*)

JANE. An unexpected pleasure for me. South Africa's so far away, and you're a busy man I'm told.
BENTLEY. A busy man who's going to have a few day's rest.
JANE. We must see that you do. Though I'm afraid our chairs could be more comfortable. Which do you prefer?
BENTLEY (*crossing to the chair* RC) This'll do for me, ma'am.

(JANE *sits in the chair* C. BENTLEY *sits in the chair* RC)

DAVID. A glass of sherry, sir?

BENTLEY. Thank you.
JANE. My husband wrote novels—period romances. He liked to live as much as possible surrounded by period pieces. Since his death we've altered very little.
BENTLEY. Do his books still sell?
JANE. No, he's forgotten—completely forgotten. At least, as a novelist.

(DAVID *moves above the table* C *with two glasses of sherry, and hovers apprehensively*)

BENTLEY. I see. Have you been a widow long?
JANE (*looking out front as though into the distance of time*) Seventeen years.
DAVID. Sherry, Mother?
JANE (*looking abstractedly*) M'm?
DAVID. Sherry?
JANE. Oh, yes. (*She takes a glass*)

(DAVID *gives the other glass to Bentley*)

BENTLEY. Thank you.

(DAVID *moves up* RC *and picks up his own drink.* JANE *sits looking into her glass*)

To our better acquaintance, Mrs Mannion.
JANE (*recovering from her abstraction*) Yes—yes, indeed.
BENTLEY. And to ours, David.

(*They drink.* DAVID *moves up* L *of the table* C)

JANE. You must be looking forward to seeing your daughter.
BENTLEY. Very much. These last few years she's spent in England, qualifying and practising, I've been lonely back there. Two short trips home—that's all she's been able to manage.
JANE. She's an attractive girl.
BENTLEY. Like her mother before her, ma'am. Yes—I'm hoping that in Maureen I'll find something of what I lost when my wife died. I'm a great believer in heredity, Mrs Mannion. My whole legal training and experience've shown me that what's bred in the bone will come out the flesh.
JANE (*reflectively*) Yes—I think there's no doubt of it.
DAVID (*a little too anxiously*) But there must be exceptions—there must be.
BENTLEY (*shaking his head*) In the long run—I'm inclined to say no, David.
DAVID. But . . .
JANE (*interrupting smoothly*) David, we've forgotten Mr Richmond's chauffeur. You'd better show him to his room.
DAVID. Oh, yes. (*He puts his glass on the chest*)
BENTLEY. I must apologize, ma'am. I didn't know you could

put him up. This trip from South Africa's a holiday he's wanted for some years—and as he fancied seeing Land's End for some unearthly reason, we're garaging the car in the village, and I've given him time off till tomorrow night. I'm sorry if it's put you to any trouble.

DAVID. Not at all, sir.

BENTLEY. I very nearly didn't bring the car. I was told your Cornish roads wouldn't do it much good.

DAVID. Some of them *are* pretty bad. (*He moves up* LC *and indicates the direction of the road*) But this one across the moor's only been finished recently. If you wanted to get to the village when I was a kid, you had to walk—and three miles pretty hard going it was, too.

BENTLEY. It must be a boon to you, then, ma'am.

JANE. I never go to the village, Mr Richmond. Since my husband died, I never go.

BENTLEY (*slightly nonplussed by her tone*) But . . .

JANE. And never shall. At least, not until . . .

MAUREEN (*off; calling*) Coo-ee! David!

DAVID. Here's Maureen.

(DAVID *exits by the windows*)

BENTLEY (*rising; his face lighting with pleasure*) Ah!

JANE (*rising and moving to Bentley*) You love Maureen?

BENTLEY. Very much, ma'am. She's my only child.

JANE. Then you must take great care of her. (*She moves to the chest and puts her glass on it*)

(BENTLEY, *with a puzzled enquiring expression, looks at Jane's back.*

MAUREEN RICHMOND *runs in by the windows. She is aged twenty-four or five, a very attractive young woman who knows her own mind. She is completely straightforward and unaffected, but warm and lovable. Her sunburn is shown off by the plain self-coloured frock she wears. She carries a small handbag.*

DAVID *follows her on.* BENTLEY *puts his glass on the table* C *and moves to* L *of the chair* C. DAVID *stands* R *of the table up* LC. JANE, *in the background, carefully watches the reunion*)

MAUREEN (*going to Bentley, and flinging her arms round his neck*) Daddy!

BENTLEY. Maureen, my darling.

(*Very slowly, the remaining sunlight starts to fade, and the part of the room down* L *becomes shadowy*)

MAUREEN. Oh, Daddy, it's been such a long time.

BENTLEY. Longer for me than for you, I think. Let me look at you.

MAUREEN (*after a pause*) Well? Pass muster?

BENTLEY (*nodding and smiling*) Pass muster.
MAUREEN. You don't look so bad yourself, either. (*Eagerly*) What's all the news?
BENTLEY. It can wait, my dear. (*He turns to Jane*) We can't expect Mrs Mannion to be very interested.
MAUREEN (*to Jane*) I'm sorry, I was forgetting.
JANE (*moving below the table* C) You'd like to be left alone together.
BENTLEY. No, please, ma'am, Maureen and I'll find plenty of time to talk later on. Do let's all sit down again.

(JANE *sits in the chair* C)

(*He moves above the table to the chair* RC) It's so long since I've been one of a family circle, I've almost forgotten what it's like.
MAUREEN (*crossing to* L *of Bentley*) Poor daddy, you're making me feel beastly—leaving you to fend for yourself all these years.
BENTLEY (*patting her arm*) I've managed. (*He sits in the chair* RC) Tell me, how are all the patients?
MAUREEN (*moving and putting her handbag on the chest*) Oh, running me off my feet. It isn't that there are so many of them, but they're so scattered. I spend far more time travelling from case to case than I do in actual doctoring.
BENTLEY. Any interesting cases?
MAUREEN (*crossing above Bentley and standing down* RC) No—just routine. The only fun's finding out what country remedy they've taken to make them well, that's made them really ill.
BENTLEY. Sounds very complicated.

(DAVID *and* MAUREEN *laugh.* JANE *breaks in*)

JANE. David, Maureen hasn't any sherry.
DAVID. Oh, sorry.
MAUREEN. Believe me, I can do with it.
DAVID. Another for you, Mother?
JANE. Thank you.
DAVID. You, sir? (*He refills Jane's glass*)
BENTLEY. Please. I haven't tasted such good sherry for years.
MAUREEN. Well, if you *will* drink South African . . .
BENTLEY. You think that's carrying patriotism a bit far?
MAUREEN (*crossing above Bentley to the table* C; *laughingly*) Yes, I do. (*She picks up Bentley's glass*) This your glass?
BENTLEY. Yes.

(MAUREEN *puts the glass on the chest*)

So professional life's dull down here, is it?
MAUREEN (*taking Jane's full glass from David*) On the whole. Though we've had a bit of excitement today. Rather dreadful it was, actually. (*She crosses above Jane to* L *of her*) You know that derelict old mineshaft out on the moor . . .

(MAUREEN *is giving the glass to* JANE, *and both are holding it, when somehow some of the sherry spills on* JANE's *dress*)

BENTLEY ⎱ (*together*) ⎰ Maureen!
MAUREEN ⎱   ⎰ Oh, I'm terribly sorry! How clumsy of me.

JANE. It doesn't matter.
MAUREEN (*turning to the door down* L) I'll get a cloth.
JANE. No, please. (*She puts the glass on the table beside her*)
BENTLEY (*rising and offering his handkerchief to* JANE) Allow me.
JANE (*taking the handkerchief*) Thank you.

(BENTLEY *resumes his seat*. DAVID *pours two more sherries*)

MAUREEN. Will it stain?
JANE (*meticulously cleaning her dress*) I don't think so. Go on with what you were saying.
MAUREEN (*moving to the chest*) Well, two kids—summer visitors —were playing near it this afternoon—and the little girl's fallen down.

(JANE *looks up*)

DAVID. Good God!
BENTLEY. How deep is it?
MAUREEN. Must be at least sixty or seventy feet.

(JANE *continues to wipe her dress*)

DAVID. Was she killed?
MAUREEN. No—they can hear her crying. (*She takes Bentley's full glass from David*) The local bobby rounded up a party of men with ropes and things—rang me to come along and stand by— and there we've all been. (*She moves to* L *of Bentley and gives him the sherry*)
BENTLEY. You haven't left them without a doctor, have you?
MAUREEN. Lord, no! Old Johnson came and relieved me.

(DAVID, *with a glass of sherry in one hand and the decanter in the other, moves above the table* C)

That's one advantage of having a partner. (*She takes a glass of sherry from David*) Thank you, darling.

(DAVID *tops up Jane's glass then returns to the chest for his own drink*)

(*She crosses above Bentley and stands down* R) He knew I'd got three or four more calls to make, so I left him there, made the calls, dashed to my digs and changed, and here I am. Late, but with pretty good reason. (*She turns the chair down* R *to face slightly up stage, and sits*)
DAVID. It's a wonder no-one's fallen down there before. The top's so overgrown it's practically hidden. (*He picks up his drink*

and moves above the table C) How long's it since it was worked, Mother?

JANE. I believe it never was a mine, David—just a shaft. Somebody hoped to find tin, or copper—then abandoned it. For many years it was half full of water—now, for some reason, it's drained away.

BENTLEY. It's strange to me, you know, that accidents like this *can* happen in England. Life's so highly organized—civilized. You'd think every possible danger to it, such as this shaft, would be safeguarded against—eliminated. Now in South Africa it's different. It's a new country.

JANE. And Cornwall's a very old country, Mr Richmond. If you stayed here long, you'd find many things stranger than that.

BENTLEY. Really?

JANE. You see, here we're still living in the shadow of our ancestors—their beliefs and practices handed down to us by word of mouth from generation to generation—ancient, savage creeds, in which the sanctity of human life had very little place.

(*The others watch Jane.* BENTLEY *is puzzled by her tone*)

(*She rises*) Would it surprise you to know—(*she moves above the table up* LC *and stands looking out in the last rays of the setting sun*) that out there on those rocks, less than a century ago, ships were deliberately lured to their destruction by the people of this very village? No, Mr Richmond—(*she turns and moves* R *of the table up* LC) in Cornwall, neither the creating of life nor the taking of it has the same importance as in newer civilizations.

MAUREEN (*breaking the atmosphere*) You're making us feel quite creepy, Mrs Mannion.

JANE. I'm sorry. (*She turns up the lamp on the table up* LC) Perhaps Mr Richmond would like to see his room before supper, David.

BENTLEY (*rising*) No, I'm quite happy, ma'am. (*He puts his glass on the chest*) Being a little nervous, and anxious to make a good impression on you and David—I tidied myself up in Camborne.

DAVID (*laughing, and turning to face Bentley*) *You* being nervous of *us*—that's wonderful. I've been in a state all day at the thought of meeting *you*.

BENTLEY (*moving to face David and putting his hand on David's shoulder; with a smile*) Well, now, I hope neither of us need worry any more. (*He sees the fly swatter on the table* C *and picks it up. Jokingly*) I see the taking of insect life has no fears for you, either, Mrs Mannion.

JANE (*moving* LC) I dislike flies, Mr Richmond.

BENTLEY. You're plagued with them here?

DAVID. Not so much since the days of D.D.T. But at one time in the summer this room was fairly buzzing with them. Bluebottles more than flies.

JANE (*breaking in quickly*) There must have been some breeding place near by.
DAVID. Anyhow, the plague's a thing of the past. And God help any solitary wanderer who gets near mother and her swatter.

(BENTLEY *laughs a little and replaces the swatter*)

MAUREEN. Where's Vanessa tonight?
BENTLEY (*crossing to* R *of Jane*) Ah, yes, I was forgetting you had a daughter.
JANE. She's in her room. She's a little shy of strangers, so I thought I wouldn't call her till supper's ready. (*She gives Bentley his handkerchief*)

(MAUREEN *rises and moves up* RC. DAVID *moves to* L *of Maureen and takes her empty glass*)

If you'll excuse me for ten minutes, I'll go and see to it. Ellen's—that's my housekeeper—prepared it all, but she's had to go to bed. She's very old, and sometimes, quite suddenly, everything gets too much for her.
MAUREEN. Like me to have a look at her?

(DAVID *puts Maureen's glass and his own on the chest*)

JANE. I don't think so, Maureen, thank you. She'll be better left alone.
MAUREEN (*moving down* RC) I'll come and give you a hand.
JANE. No, please. You and David must want to talk to your father. (*She turns towards the door down* L) And there's very little to do.

(BENTLEY *moves to the door down* L *and opens it*)

(*Moving down* L) It's only cold salmon and salad.
BENTLEY. It sounds delightful.

(JANE *goes out*. BENTLEY *closes the door, moves to* LC *offering his cigar case to David*)

Cigar, David?
DAVID. No, thank you, sir. (*He moves above the table* C, *taking a cigarette from the box*) I'll have one of these, if you don't mind.

(BENTLEY *moves to the table up* LC *and cuts his cigar*)

(*Offering the box to Maureen*) You, Maureen?
MAUREEN (*moving to him*) Thank you. (*She takes a cigarette*)

(DAVID *lights Maureen's cigarette*)

BENTLEY. Well, now.
DAVID (*lighting his cigarette*) How do you feel, sir, about the engagement?

BENTLEY (*moving above the chair* LC, *lighting his cigar*) I'm not sure, David. You see, Maureen's told me so little about you.
MAUREEN. I wanted to wait till you'd met David.
BENTLEY. Yes, so you said in your letters. Well, now we *are* meeting.

(MAUREEN *sits on the left arm of the chair* RC, *with her back half turned to the audience*)

DAVID. And you don't approve?
BENTLEY. Come now, David, I may be old-fashioned in some things, but I don't imagine that nowadays a father's approval, or disapproval makes much difference to a young couple who want to get married.
MAUREEN. It makes a difference to me, Daddy, you know it does.
BENTLEY. But you're of age, my dear. I couldn't stop you, even if I wanted to. (*He puts the spent match in the ashtray on the table up* LC)
DAVID. We'd still like you to be happy about it.
BENTLEY. Is there any reason I shouldn't be?
DAVID. Well—I hope not.
BENTLEY (*after a look at David over his shoulder*) H'm. (*He looks around the room*) This is an interesting place you've got here, David.
DAVID. Yes.
BENTLEY. Rather large to keep up, isn't it?
DAVID. Some of the rooms are closed.
BENTLEY. And your mother runs it with just one servant?
DAVID. Yes.
BENTLEY. She must be a very capable woman.

(MAUREEN *crosses and stubs out her cigarette in the ashtray on the dresser*)

She's Cornish, I take it?
DAVID. Yes.
BENTLEY. Lived here all her life?
DAVID. No—she was born near a little village on the moors round Bodmin.
BENTLEY. But she went away from Cornwall to school, I suppose.
DAVID. No. (*He nervously flicks his cigarette ash into the ashtray on the table* C) Actually, by birth, she's a peasant.
BENTLEY. Really? (*He moves below the chair* LC *and looks towards the door down* L) I'd never have thought it. (*He sits in the chair* LC) Is she self-educated?
DAVID. Not exactly.
MAUREEN (*moving down* R) Daddy, it's David we want to talk about, not . . .

DAVID (*moving to* L *of the chair* RC) Your father's got to know, Maureen.
MAUREEN. But . . .
BENTLEY. Know what, David?

(MAUREEN *sits in the chair down* R)

DAVID (*moving below the table* C) Well, I don't quite know how, or where to begin.
BENTLEY (*reassuringly*) Take it easily.
DAVID. You must have noticed mother's—well—she's got rather a—an odd manner.
BENTLEY. Yes.
DAVID (*moving* LC *and facing Bentley*) And as Maureen's father, you've a right to know why.
BENTLEY. I think I have—yes.

(*The sun has set and it is dark outside the windows. With the warmth of the sun's rays gone, the room has taken on a cold, rather sinister aspect*)

DAVID (*moving and stubbing out his cigarette in the ashtray on the chest*) I can't say what I'm going to tell you is true, word for word. I've only picked it up here and there, a little from her, but most of it from old Johnson, who knew my father better and longer than anyone else. (*He moves to the chair* C) Except for one incident, no-one knows much of her early life, but when she was about twenty she came to Marjizal—that's the village here—looking for work. But everyone turned her from their doors.
BENTLEY. Why?
DAVID. I'll come to that later if I may. She was practically starving when one day, on the moor, my father found her. He was a strange man—I don't know how to describe him exactly . . .
MAUREEN. Eccentric?
DAVID (*turning to her*) Yes. (*He circles below the table* C *and stands up* R *of it*) One day on top of the world, the next morose, hard and cruel.
BENTLEY. Cruel!
DAVID (*turning to him*) I'm afraid so—yes.
BENTLEY. Go on.
DAVID (*moving below the chair* RC) He brought her home here and she became his housekeeper. But she also became a sort of guinea-pig for him to experiment on.
BENTLEY. How d'you mean—experiment?
DAVID (*sitting in the chair* RC) He fancied himself as a sort of Pygmalion with her as Galatea, and turned her, at least superficially, into a lady. And all the time he dissected her, recording her emotions.
BENTLEY. Poor woman.
DAVID. At times she felt she couldn't bear it any longer, but

when she tried to show no emotion at all, he goaded her until she did.
BENTLEY. Her life must have been hell!
DAVID. I don't really love her . . .
MAUREEN (*rising*) David!
DAVID. Not as much as a son should—but she is my mother, and when I think what she must have gone through . . .
MAUREEN (*going to David and putting her arm around him*) Don't go on, darling.
BENTLEY (*rising*) I've got to know the rest, Maureen.

(MAUREEN *moves and stands by the dresser*)

DAVID. For some reason—possibly he was afraid of losing her—or wanted someone to look after him in his old age—he was over sixty—he married her, and later, I was born.

(BENTLEY *moves slowly to* R *of the table up* LC)

That was when Ellen came here. For eight years I was well looked after, but always without any sort of affection. Then I went away to prep school. Mother wrote to me every week. The first holidays I couldn't come home—I had measles. The second holidays I had to stay away because father was ill. In my third term I had a letter—late one night my father had gone out walking on the moors, and hadn't come back. He'd disappeared.
BENTLEY (*turning*) Disappeared!
DAVID. He's never been seen again.
BENTLEY (*moving down* LC) No traces at all?
DAVID. Nothing.
BENTLEY. There must have been *some* clue, surely?
DAVID (*shaking his head*) He'd been ill spasmodically for something like three months. But what can have happened nobody knows.

(BENTLEY, *thinking hard, moves unobtrusively below the chair* LC *and stands up* L *of it*)

Johnson thought at first it was one of his devilish tricks—just to worry mother. But the people in the village didn't think so. Within a month, the whispering began—locally at first, and quietly. Then it began to spread—round the coast, across the moors, till everyone was saying—*openly saying* . . .
BENTLEY. Yes?
DAVID. That my mother had poisoned my father and disposed of the body.
BENTLEY (*moving* LC) Without any grounds? Any foundation?
DAVID (*quietly*) No—there were grounds. In Cornish eyes—good grounds.
BENTLEY. Which were?

DAVID (*rising*) I told you when mother first came to Marjizal, all doors were shut in her face.

BENTLEY. Yes.

DAVID (*moving up* R *of the table* C; *not looking at Bentley*) She was treated like that because word had got round who she was.

BENTLEY. Who was she?

DAVID. She was the daughter of a woman who was tried—(*the phrases come in jerks*) for murdering her husband—by arsenic poisoning.

(BENTLEY, *horrified, looks at Maureen.*

JANE *enters quietly down* L *and stands just inside the doorway.* MAUREEN, *seeing Jane, takes a slow step forward.* BENTLEY, *realizing from Maureen's movement that someone has come in, turns sharply and looks at* JANE, *who holds his look*)

JANE. Did I startle you, Mr Richmond?

BENTLEY. No, ma'am, no. (*He moves and stubs out his cigar in the ashtray on the table up* LC)

(JANE *looks at David, sensing what has happened, moves to the gong and beats a long roll on it, then carefully hangs up the beater.* BENTLEY *unobtrusively watches Jane.* DAVID *moves to Maureen*)

JANE. Supper won't be a moment. (*She crosses to the table* C *and picks up her glass of sherry*) I expect David's been telling you something about us all.

BENTLEY (*moving down slightly; quietly*) Something—yes—ma'am.

JANE. We must see you get the chance of another talk after supper. (*She puts her glass on the chest*)

BENTLEY. I'd appreciate it.

(VANESSA MANNION *enters down the stairs; she is aged nearly seventeen, but looks and behaves much younger. She is very slight with a pale, elfin face, large eyes, and very fair hair. There is a fragile and rather fey quality about her. She is simply dressed in a white summer frock.* JANE *looks up at Vanessa, and smiles for the first time*)

JANE (*holding out her hand to Vanessa*) Ah, Vanessa, come and meet Mr Richmond, darling. (*She puts her arm around Vanessa and leads her to Bentley*) This is my daughter, Vanessa.

VANESSA (*holding out her hand; gravely and rather like a child on its best party manners*) How do you do, Mr Richmond?

BENTLEY. Very well, my dear. (*He shakes hands*) And very pleased to meet you.

VANESSA (*simply*) Thank you.

JANE (*leading Vanessa to the chair* RC) Sit down a minute, darling.

MAUREEN. Hello, Van.

(BENTLEY *sits in the chair* LC)

VANESSA. Hello, Maureen (*She sits in the chair* RC)

SCENE I TELL-TALE MURDER

(*The telephone off gives a series of faint, long rings*)

JANE (*faintly surprised*) There's the telephone, David.
DAVID (*crossing above the table* C *to the door down* L) I'll answer it.

(JANE *stands above the chair* RC, *and gently plays with Vanessa's hair*. VANESSA *makes no sign, but seems mutely to dislike it*.

DAVID *exits down* L)

JANE. You know, Mr Richmond, I could never let Vanessa go away from me, as you let Maureen. I didn't even let her go to school. She had a governess—a French governess. She speaks French beautifully.
BENTLEY. And how do you like Cornwall, Miss Vanessa?
VANESSA. It frightens me.
BENTLEY. Frightens you?
JANE. She reads too much.
VANESSA. Not the country, but the people.
BENTLEY (*a little surprised*) Your own folk?
MAUREEN. You're a changeling, aren't you, Van?
JANE (*harshly*) Vanessa is Cornish. She has these dreams—these fancies—*because* she's Cornish. She'll grow out of them.
BENTLEY. As you have, Mrs Mannion?
JANE. Yes, Mr Richmond, as I have.

(DAVID, *looking rather serious, enters down* L)

DAVID (*crossing above Bentley to* LC) Mother, could we have supper now? I've got to go out immediately afterwards.
JANE (*looking keenly at him*) Is anything wrong, David?
DAVID (*laughing reassuringly*) No, no. Why should there be?
JANE. You . . .
DAVID (*turning quickly to Bentley*) I'm sorry, Mr Richmond, on your first night, but I'll be back as soon as I can.
BENTLEY. Don't worry about me, David.
JANE (*moving below the table* C; *to Bentley*) Then shall we go in, Mr Richmond?

(BENTLEY *rises and moves to the door down* L)

The dining-room's in the new part of the house—relatively new, that is—late Georgian . . .

(BENTLEY *and* JANE *exit down* L)

MAUREEN (*overlapping; rising and moving to Vanessa*) Come on, Van.

(VANESSA *rises and crosses to the door down* L. MAUREEN *follows her*. DAVID *moves down* LC)

I love supper in your house. All that candlelight . . .

(VANESSA *exits down* L)

DAVID. Maureen!
MAUREEN (*turning and moving to David*) Yes, darling?
DAVID. Kiss me.
MAUREEN (*laughing remonstratively*) David!

(DAVID *kisses her*)

Really, Mr Mannion!
DAVID (*tensely*) Whatever happens, you wouldn't give me up, Maureen, would you?
MAUREEN (*simply*) I love you, David.
DAVID. Yes. But promise me—nothing'll stop us getting married, will it?
MAUREEN (*gently amused at his urgency*) What . . . ?
DAVID. Promise!
MAUREEN (*suddenly serious*) I promise.

(DAVID, *in great relief, buries his head on her shoulder*)

VANESSA (*off; calling*) Maureen.
MAUREEN (*breaking from David and calling*) Coming. (*She smiles up at David and fondles his cheek*) What a strange boy you are.
MAUREEN *and* DAVID *move towards the door down* L *as—*

the CURTAIN *falls*

SCENE 2

SCENE—*The same. After supper, the same evening.*

When the CURTAIN *rises, the window curtains are still open, the night has become moonlit, and there are occasional flashes of distant summer lightning. A tray of coffee things is on the table up* LC. VANESSA *is sitting, quite still, on the pouffe, facing up to* MAUREEN, *who is standing up* R *of the table up* LC. MAUREEN *is holding an empty coffee cup and saucer, and is looking out of the windows. She is a little tensed up, and probably rather tired.*

MAUREEN. I wish that storm'd come. This heavy heat's frightful.
VANESSA. Yes.
MAUREEN. It's like the Transvaal—the air full of subdued rustling—but you can't hear it.
VANESSA. Did David tell you where he was going?
MAUREEN. No. (*She puts her cup and saucer on the tray*)
VANESSA. He hardly ate any supper.
MAUREEN (*moving* LC) I'm worried, Van.
VANESSA. What about?
MAUREEN. There's an "atmosphere" here tonight. Can't *you*

sense it? (*She sits in the chair* LC) We're all *saying* one thing—and thinking something else.

VANESSA (*rising and moving a little up stage of Maureen*) It's this house. Get away from it, Maureen. Get David away from it. Then . . . (*She breaks off*)

(JANE *enters at the top of the stairs, carrying a lighted candle in a heavy brass candlestick.* VANESSA *turns, taking a step backwards, so that she is up* L *of the chair* LC, *facing Jane*)

JANE (*raising the candlestick and speaking off*) There are two twisted stairs there, Mr Richmond—be careful.

(BENTLEY *enters at the top of the stairs. He is smoking a cigar*)

BENTLEY. It certainly is a fascinating place.
JANE (*coming down the stairs*) The candle lent enchantment.

(BENTLEY *follows Jane down the stairs*)

In the daytime it's different. This house was meant to be lived in only at night.
BENTLEY. But it's a museum piece. (*He crosses and stands up* L *of the chair* C) Elizabethan—Stuart—Georgian—Early Victorian . . .
JANE (*moving up* R *of the table* C) And then we stop.
VANESSA (*moving to the coffee tray*) Black coffee, or white, Mr Richmond?
BENTLEY. Black, please.

(VANESSA *pours coffee for Jane and Bentley*)

JANE. Each owner added something—something that would make the place seem more his own.
BENTLEY. And what have you added?
JANE. Me? Nothing. (*Slowly she blows out the candle, then puts it on the dresser*) There's just the money now to live here—the three of us together—nothing to spare. (*She crosses to the chair* C) My husband had these windows put in and was intending to add a room on the south-east corner. He was to build it himself, with just a man to help him. All the materials were here—and then . . . (*She makes a gesture*)
BENTLEY. He disappeared.
JANE (*looking at Bentley and realizing he has heard the story*) Yes.
VANESSA. Sugar, Mr Richmond?
BENTLEY. No, thank you. (*He takes his coffee from Vanessa*)

(JANE *sits in the chair* C)

(*He crosses above the table* C *to* R *of it*) It seems a strange place to build such a house—so far from everywhere.

(VANESSA *hands a cup of coffee to Jane*)

JANE. There was a reason—a good reason.

(Vanessa *stands* R *of the table up* LC)

Bentley. Oh?
Jane. Smuggling.
Bentley (*sitting in the chair* RC) Of course—yes.
Maureen. So *that's* why they had those hiding-places under the flagstones of the floors.
Jane (*looking over her left shoulder at Maureen*) How did *you* know?
Maureen. David told me Ellen used to frighten him when he was naughty, saying she'd put him down one and nobody'd ever find him.
Jane. Did she!
Maureen. One day we went round tapping all the floors with a mallet, trying out where they were. But it wasn't any good.
Jane. No, they were blocked up long before I came to "Porthenis".
Vanessa (*moving to* L *of Jane*) Can I go out, Mother?
Jane. If you like.
Vanessa. It's so—airless—in here.
Jane. There'll be no breeze on the moor tonight.
Maureen (*rising*) *I* could do with a stroll. We'll go on the cliffs, shall we, Van?
Vanessa (*moving to the windows*) Yes, yes—anywhere.
Jane (*rising, cup in hand, and turning to face the windows*) Not too far. There's a storm around.
Maureen. You don't mind, Daddy?
Bentley. Of course not.
Maureen (*moving to the windows*) Just ten minutes, eh, Van?
Vanessa. Yes.

(Vanessa *and* Maureen *exit by the windows*)

Jane. Vanessa's very young for her age.
Bentley. She's charming.
Jane (*moving to Bentley*) Let me take your cup.
Bentley (*handing his cup to Jane*) Thank you.

(Jane *puts both cups on the tray.* Bentley *watches her curiously*)

Jane (*looking out of the windows*) The lightning's very far away.
Bentley. Will it get nearer, d'you think?
Jane. It may.
Bentley. I'm sorry David had to go out.
Jane (*moving below the chair* C *and taking her sewing from the basket*) I'm afraid I interrupted your talk before supper.
Bentley. Yes, ma'am, at a rather vital stage. It has left me in a state of suspense.
Jane. Supposing that suspense had lasted seventeen years, Mr Richmond. Could you have borne it?

BENTLEY. It would need great courage.
JANE (*sitting slowly in the chair* C) Yes.
BENTLEY. You have my sympathy. It must have influenced your whole life—guided your every action.
JANE. Possibly. I don't know.

(BENTLEY *looks at Jane, trying to gauge her sincerity*)

I'm not a clever woman. I act instinctively. I haven't the brains to work out what I should, or shouldn't do—I can't try to guide events. I can only react to them when they happen. (*She sews*)
BENTLEY (*studying the end of his cigar*) And this particular event —this proposed marriage—what are your reactions to that?
JANE. It would be a very good thing for David.
BENTLEY. And for my daughter? For me?
JANE. I don't know you well enough to say.
BENTLEY. But you're willing it should take place.
JANE. I have no choice.
BENTLEY. But are you willing?
JANE. Yes.
BENTLEY. Regardless of the effect it may have on Maureen?
JANE. What effect?
BENTLEY. Mrs Mannion—you are a woman under suspicion. I know how easily such things arise—and how easily the suspicion may be wrong . . .
JANE. Do you suspect me?
BENTLEY. I can hardly say until I know the answer to a question I wasn't able to ask earlier on.
JANE. What question?
BENTLEY. Your mother, David tells me, was tried for her life.
JANE (*intent on her sewing*) Yes.
BENTLEY. On a charge of murdering her husband by arsenic poisoning.
JANE. Yes.
BENTLEY. What was the jury's verdict?
JANE (*very smoothly*) My mother was acquitted, Mr Richmond.
BENTLEY (*after a pause*) I'm very relieved to hear it; Mrs Mannion.
JANE. It makes such a difference to you?
BENTLEY. Every difference in the world. I know that, once the criminal's caught, he seldom escapes justice, and if your mother'd been found guilty, I'd 've *had* to try to make Maureen break with David—and that would have been very painful for all of us. (*He rises*) I can't tell you, ma'am, the load you've lifted from my mind.
JANE (*nodding towards the chest; with wry humour*) The whisky's there.

(BENTLEY, *laughing a little, moves to the chest and pours a drink for himself*)

BENTLEY. Something for you?
JANE. No, thank you.
BENTLEY (*picking up his glass and moving down* LC) To your son and my daughter, Mrs Mannion. (*He drinks*)
JANE. You're giving them your blessing?
BENTLEY. I think so—yes.
JANE. In spite of what you just said?
BENTLEY. What was that?
JANE. That I'm a woman under suspicion.
BENTLEY (*crossing to the chair* RC) I can't afford to take too much notice of that—not after what you've told me about your mother. (*He sits*) My daughter's happiness, you see, ma'am, means more to me than anything else in the world. How can I jeopardize it because of rumours which now, probably, can never be proved?
JANE. I see.
BENTLEY. They can, of course, be disproved.
JANE. How?
BENTLEY. Simply enough—an action for slander.
JANE. Put myself in the pillory again?
BENTLEY. But think, ma'am, isn't it worth it?
JANE. No!
BENTLEY. There's a great deal at stake.
JANE. Too much. I *can't* go through it all again. After my mother's trial, I didn't really mind being shunned by the people at home—it was understandable in a way. But when I tried to face up to it—work out a new life for myself—d'you know what happened? I was driven from village to village—victimized—hunted! You don't realize what it means to have everyone's hand against you.
BENTLEY. I *have* come across cases . . .
JANE. But *still*—you yourself can't know what it means.
BENTLEY (*agreeing*) No.
JANE. That's why, when my husband disappeared—when they all said history was repeating itself—I shut myself up here. I wouldn't face it then—I can't face it now.
BENTLEY. Not if I help you—as I'd be glad to?
JANE. It'd be no good.
BENTLEY. But don't you see you owe it to your *children* to clear yourself?
JANE. I *can't* clear myself.
BENTLEY. Why not?
JANE. Because of the past.
BENTLEY. But . . .
JANE. Your thoughts have been so occupied with the possibility of murder, you've overlooked the fact there may be other family traits almost as bad.
BENTLEY. How do you mean?

JANE. I think you should know my father was a very violent man. I spent my childhood in fear—for my own life, and my mother's. And as I grew older it wasn't only for my *life* I feared. I can hear it now—the shambling, drunken step—the lurch against the door—I can feel his hands, clutching and tearing. If it hadn't been for my mother, God knows what would have happened to me.

BENTLEY (*suspiciously*) What's that to do . . . ?

JANE (*emphatically*) The stock is rotten, Mr Richmond, don't touch it.

BENTLEY. You told me you were willing David should marry. Is that the truth?

JANE (*nervously putting away her sewing in the basket*) I don't know.

BENTLEY (*rising and putting his glass on the table* C) You don't want him to, do you. But you'd rather I stopped it than you. (*He moves up* L *of the table* C) That's why you're telling me this—that's what you're trying to trick me into, isn't it?

(JANE *picks up her basket, rises agitatedly, crosses to the dresser and puts the basket on it*)

JANE. I'm only trying to tell you the truth.

BENTLEY (*moving above the table* C) What *is* the truth! What are the *facts!* One thing only's been legally proved—your mother's innocence.

JANE (*turning*) But *was* she innocent?

BENTLEY. Be careful what you're saying, Mrs Mannion. It's one thing putting me off with sordid stories of your childhood which may or may not be true. It's a different thing to accuse your own mother of murder.

JANE (*moving above the chair* RC) I don't accuse. Or condemn. I loved her the more for it.

BENTLEY. Mrs Mannion!

JANE. My mother poisoned my father. I knew she was doing it, and I was glad.

BENTLEY. D'you realize . . . ?

JANE. But whatever my *mother* may have done—however guilty I am in shielding her—as far as my *husband's* concerned, I'm innocent.

(*There is a momentary pause.*

DAVID *enters down* L. *He is too preoccupied to notice the tension.* BENTLEY *moves to the chest*)

DAVID. Hello, Mother.

JANE (*hardly audible*) Hello, David.

DAVID. I've just come from the village. (*He moves up* R *of the chair* LC) They got that kid safely out of the mineshaft—but—they got something else as well. A body—a *man's* body.

JANE. Well?

DAVID. They think it's father's.

JANE *stares at David for a moment.* BENTLEY *looks at Jane.* JANE, *with a slight intake of breath, turns to hold on to the back of the chair* RC, *and stares out front as—*

the CURTAIN *falls*

ACT II

SCENE—*The same. The following evening about 9 o'clock.*

When the CURTAIN *rises, the window curtains and the windows are open, and outside the night is moonlit. All the lamps are lit.* BENTLEY *is seated in the chair* RC, *reading. He wears horn-rimmed spectacles. He turns a page, and is intent on the book.* ELLEN *enters stealthily at the top of the stairs, and peers down at Bentley. She turns to go but makes a slight noise, and disturbs him.* ELLEN *exits at the top of the stairs.* BENTLEY *looks round but is just too late to see her. He rises, moves* L *of his chair and looks towards the stairs.*

BENTLEY. Hello, there! (*He pauses*) That you, Vanessa?

(MAUREEN *enters by the windows. She wears a different frock*)

MAUREEN (*moving* LC) Who're you calling?
BENTLEY (*turning*) I don't know. A ghost presumably. (*He crosses to Maureen*) I was sitting here reading, and I'll swear someone came to the top of these stairs.
MAUREEN. Ellen probably. She's a bit cracked.
BENTLEY. No reason she should make me think I am.
MAUREEN (*crossing down* RC) Where is everybody?
BENTLEY (*pocketing his spectacles*) There was a phone call from St Ives about five o'clock. David's taken his mother there.
MAUREEN. Not to see the body?
BENTLEY (*moving to the chair* LC) I doubt if there's much body left to see.
MAUREEN. There isn't.
BENTLEY (*sitting in the chair* LC) But someone's got to identify it.
MAUREEN. Johnson was called in to see it last night—before it was taken to St Ives.
BENTLEY. Any recognizable features?
MAUREEN. Not as far as he was concerned.
BENTLEY. Clothing?
MAUREEN. Shreds. Shoes were pretty well preserved.
BENTLEY. Any internal organs?

(MAUREEN *glances quickly at him, then away again*)

MAUREEN. Yes—parts. Most useful thing was a signet ring on the little finger of the right hand.
BENTLEY. Enough to go on.
MAUREEN (*moving up* RC) What have you been doing with yourself?

BENTLEY. I had a look round the village this morning—met one or two interesting old characters. Quite talkative they were, too.
MAUREEN (*with constraint*) Oh.
BENTLEY. How long have you known Mrs Mannion? Nine months?
MAUREEN. Getting on.
BENTLEY. Have you managed to form any opinion of her?
MAUREEN. I've tried to—but I've changed my mind so many times I—(*she makes a gesture of helplessness*) just haven't an opinion. (*She moves below the chair* C) To begin with I couldn't help feeling there was something—(*she sits*) evil about her. That closed face—the silent *watchfulness* of her. Then—when I learnt more about her—I began to think. Almost any woman with her background—living in her circumstances—*would* keep her face like a mask—would *have* every *right* to be bitter—would have *cause* to be wary and watchful. None of it may be natural to her. She may be a perfectly ordinary woman that circumstances have made seem—sinister, I suppose is the word.
BENTLEY. Yes.
MAUREEN. I've chopped and changed between those two opinions, and still can't make up my mind.
BENTLEY (*rising*) You say sometimes you thought there was something "evil" about her. Did you ever think it went further than that? That possibly she *may* be a criminal—a poisoner?
MAUREEN. No, I—I've never seriously thought that.
BENTLEY. H'm! (*He crosses down* RC) D'you know what Mannion's symptoms were? He'd been ill quite a bit, hadn't he?
MAUREEN. Johnson told me his heart had been groggy for years. Then he began to get severe pains in the stomach . . .
BENTLEY. What was Johnson's diagnosis?
MAUREEN. Well, he's an awful old dodderer—he hasn't any definite opinion—except that there's no question of poison.
BENTLEY. And what about you—do *you* feel there's no possibility?
MAUREEN. There's easily the possibility—but is there the likelihood?
BENTLEY. I just don't know, Maureen.
MAUREEN. But think, Daddy. With her mother's case known throughout Cornwall, if she'd wanted to murder her husband, would she have chosen poison? And how else *could* she have done it? Short of brute force.
BENTLEY (*ruminatively*) There *have* been women stranglers. A quick jerk with a strong cord—suffocation—or a broken neck.
MAUREEN (*rising*) I don't believe it!
BENTLEY. You don't want to believe it!
MAUREEN. No, I don't. (*She moves up* L *of the chair* C) The whole thing's a ghastly set of coincidences.
BENTLEY. Well—perhaps you're right. (*He moves to the chest and*

puts his book out of sight on it) And as long as *you're* perfectly happy in your mind . . .

(MAUREEN *does not reply*)

(*He turns*) You are—aren't you?

MAUREEN (*reluctantly*) Well—perhaps I'm not—altogether. I may as well tell you—you'll only find it out from someone else. There *is* one thing I *can't* get over.

BENTLEY (*moving up* R *of the table* C) Yes—well?

MAUREEN. She didn't report her husband's disappearance for nearly forty-eight hours.

BENTLEY. Forty-eight hours!

MAUREEN. Rather a long time, isn't it?

BENTLEY. What reason did she give?

MAUREEN. Well—(*she sits in the chair* LC) apparently she just wasn't *worried* about him being missing.

BENTLEY (*moving down* R *of the table* C) Look, Maureen, we've got to get this thing sorted out.

MAUREEN. But why *now?*

BENTLEY. We've got to *start* now. The discovery of this body *may* be the beginning of a lot of trouble.

MAUREEN. Or the end of it.

BENTLEY. Suppose it's the beginning—suppose Mrs Mannion *is* involved—you'll have to think very seriously of breaking this engagement.

MAUREEN (*rising; distressed*) But, Daddy—I can't!

BENTLEY (*moving below the chair* C) You've got to consider the future, my dear.

MAUREEN (*going to him*) It's *my* future, isn't it?

BENTLEY. And the future of your children, too—don't forget that.

MAUREEN (*crossing below Bentley to* R *of him*) Daddy—please!

BENTLEY. And if *you* won't see it, *I've* got to see for you.

MAUREEN (*turning*) See *what?* At the moment you've got nothing to go on—absolutely nothing.

BENTLEY (*moving up* LC) I've got quite enough.

MAUREEN. If this body *is* Richard Mannion's, within a week we'll know . . .

BENTLEY (*turning*) I know one thing *now*, Maureen. I'm not letting you marry this woman's son, without putting up a damned hard fight to prevent it.

MAUREEN. It won't be any good, Daddy. I'm marrying David.

BENTLEY (*moving up* L *of the table* C) But if I bring you proof positive?

MAUREEN. Very well! Bring it me.

BENTLEY. All right.

MAUREEN (*turning away and trying not to cry*) Oh, Daddy, *why* did it have to be like this?

BENTLEY (*moving to Maureen and putting his arm around her*) There, there.
MAUREEN (*her head on his chest*) Why couldn't I have fallen in love, and everything been happy, and straightforward, and uncomplicated?
BENTLEY (*gently*) Have a good cry.
MAUREEN (*with a touch of humour through her tears*) I don't think I can stop myself.

(VANESSA *enters and comes down the stairs*)

VANESSA (*moving above the table* C) What is it? What's wrong?

(BENTLEY *crosses above Maureen to* R)

MAUREEN (*crossing down* LC) It's nothing, Van.
VANESSA (*moving quickly down* RC) Tell me, please. Is mother . . .
MAUREEN. No. Van, she's all right. I'm just being a bit silly, that's all.
VANESSA. It's awful—the waiting, isn't it?
BENTLEY. It'll soon be over, Miss Vanessa.
VANESSA (*looking at Bentley; wide-eyed*) Yes. Or it'll never be over. (*Hopelessly*) And then . . .
MAUREEN. Don't you see, Daddy? You just can't *do* it.

(BENTLEY *turns up* R)

VANESSA (*looking from one to the other*) What are you talking about?
MAUREEN (*moving to Vanessa and leading her to the chair* C) Come and sit down, Van.
VANESSA (*looking at the chair*) No—not there. (*She moves quickly to the chair* LC *and sits*) I'll sit here.
MAUREEN (*trying to break the atmosphere*) Now let's all be sensible and . . .
VANESSA. Why's Mr Richmond upset?
MAUREEN (*kneeling* R *of Vanessa*) Only because I am—and you are.
VANESSA. I'm sorry.
BENTLEY (*moving below the table* C) I'm sorry, too, Vanessa. I've come at an unhappy time for you all.
VANESSA. I'm glad you're here, though. (*She smiles confidingly*) I—I trust you.
MAUREEN (*rising; her back half turned to Vanessa, trying to hide her emotion*) Darling Van.
VANESSA. You're a doctor, Maureen——

(MAUREEN *turns to her*)

—you can tell me. If it is my father—this body—will they be able to say if he—if he was poisoned?
MAUREEN. I think so—yes, Van.

VANESSA. I see.
BENTLEY (*sitting in the chair* C; *gently*) But surely—*you* don't think he *could* have been poisoned, do you?
MAUREEN. Daddy!
BENTLEY. Do you, Vanessa?
VANESSA (*simply*) I don't know.
MAUREEN. How can you say such a thing, Van. If you love your mother . . .
VANESSA. I do love her, Maureen, of course I do, but—(*she looks down and shudders slightly*) she frightens me.
BENTLEY. Why?
VANESSA. I can't say why. It's just that . . . (*She breaks off and listens*) She's coming.
MAUREEN (*listening*) I didn't hear . . .
VANESSA. Up the path.
MAUREEN (*moving to the windows and looking off*) She's right.
VANESSA (*rising and moving to* L *of Bentley*) You won't tell mother?
BENTLEY. No, of course not.

(*There is a slight pause.* VANESSA *moves slightly up* LC *and stands waiting.*
JANE *enters by the windows. She is wearing a dark grey, severely cut coat over her long dress, a fine woollen shawl over her head and thrown over her shoulder, and gloves. She seems tired and old, and walks slowly.*
DAVID *follows Jane on. He is wearing a dark suit.* BENTLEY *rises*)

JANE. Ah, Maureen.
MAUREEN. Hello, Mrs Mannion.
JANE (*moving to* L *of Vanessa*) Vanessa. (*She fondles Vanessa's hair*) How golden your hair shines in the lamplight. (*She slowly removes her gloves and crosses down* RC)

(VANESSA *stands up* RC)

(*To Bentley*) You must forgive me neglecting you all day, Mr Richmond, but earlier on I wasn't well, and then, later—(*she shrugs slightly*) I had no alternative.
BENTLEY (*gravely and courteously*) I quite understand.
JANE (*moving up* R *of the table* C) Do please sit down.
BENTLEY. Thank you. (*He crosses and sits in the chair* LC)

(DAVID *links his arm in* MAUREEN'S *and stands with her up* LC.
JANE *puts her gloves on the table* C, *and unwinds the shawl from her head, also putting it on the table*)

JANE (*in a tired, rather drab voice*) You know—I'd almost forgotten what a town looks like. It was a strange feeling—seeing so many houses, and shops, and people, too. All quite unaware that anything unusual was happening. And I don't suppose they'd have cared much if they did know. It wasn't sensational enough—that a woman who'd lived shut away from the world should have been forced out of her seclusion to walk amongst them again. But they'll come running quickly enough to stare and point—yes, *and* throw stones—if anything sensational *does* happen.

BENTLEY. Is there any fear of that, Mrs Mannion?

JANE. There's always fear of it, Mr Richmond. (*She moves down* RC) It's a fear we'll have to live with for the next few days.

MAUREEN (*alarmed*) What's happened, Mrs Mannion?

JANE (*moving to the chair* C *and sitting*) They questioned me—and questioned me. Oh, they were very cunning. To anyone else they'd have shown what remained, first—but not to me. Oh, no. They wanted *me* to tell *them* what Richard was wearing—what colour his shoes were—what size he took. Do you remember, Mr Richmond, what size shoes your wife wore?

BENTLEY. No, I can't say I do.

JANE. They expected me to know. I suppose I should have—I cleaned them often enough. But at last they showed me—the shoes, the buttons, the mildewed shreds of clothing, the ring.

BENTLEY. And did you identify them?

JANE (*not looking at him*) Yes. It *is* my husband's body.

BENTLEY. Did you—forgive me if this is painful to you—did you see the actual remains of your husband?

(JANE, *for the first time, shows signs of distress. Her face crumples slightly*)

JANE (*in a low voice*) Yes. It was horrible.

DAVID (*crossing to Jane*) Don't upset yourself, Mother.

JANE. How can I help it? We read in the Bible, ashes to ashes, dust to dust. But this wasn't dust. It was . . .

VANESSA (*moving quickly down* R *of the table* C) Don't, Mother, please!

JANE (*pulling herself together*) I'm sorry, Vanessa, I'd forgotten you were there.

(VANESSA *moves to* R *of the chair* RC)

DAVID (*moving to the chest*) Shall I get you a drink?

JANE. No, thank you, I'll be all right.

BENTLEY. And there's no doubt in your mind that this was your husband?

JANE. None whatever.

BENTLEY. What made you so sure?

JANE. I suppose—really, it was the ring, the ring that made me certain.

BENTLEY. Then surely everything must be pretty simple and straightforward.

JANE. I don't know.

BENTLEY. But at any rate, there's no reason to fear any sensational developments.
DAVID (*moving up* R *of the table* C) Mother's upset because of something they told her. I tried to get her to see it isn't important, but she's worrying about it.
BENTLEY. May we know what it is?
JANE. Just as we were leaving, they told me something I hadn't noticed.
DAVID. You couldn't have been expected to.
JANE. All the bones of my husband's body were—intact, except the neck. The neck was broken.
MAUREEN (*involuntarily*) Broken!

(MAUREEN's *eyes meet* BENTLEY's)

JANE. How could that have happened?
DAVID (*moving down* RC) I've told you, Mother, in the fall.
BENTLEY. But I thought the shaft was full of water.
DAVID (*looking quickly at Bentley; slowly*) Yes—yes, of course—it was.
MAUREEN. *Half* full.
BENTLEY (*rising and moving behind his chair*) There's probably some simple explanation. When is the inquest?
DAVID. It'll open tomorrow, and be adjourned. Probably for a week. (*He crosses below Jane to* L *of her*) God, what a week it'll be, too. Uncertainty—suspense—it'll be hell.
JANE (*turning on him*) Why, David? *Why* will it be hell?
DAVID (*uncomfortably*) Well—you know. The investigations.
JANE. Why should they worry you?
DAVID. I only meant . . .
JANE. I know what you meant, David. You're afraid.
VANESSA (*moving below the chair* RC; *distressed*) Mother!
JANE. And you, Vanessa, are you afraid, too?
VANESSA (*turning away down* R) I can't help it.
JANE. So—(*she rises wearily*) even my own children suspect me.

(VANESSA *turns*)

DAVID. No, Mother!
JANE. The only poison here is in your *mind*, David—yours and Vanessa's.
DAVID (*with a step towards Jane*) But . . .
JANE (*moving down* R *of the table* C) Oh, it's not your fault. I'm the only one to blame. I've become so many things I wish I weren't. But I'm still human. (*She turns and looks at David*) And you're my children—(*she turns to Vanessa*) and I love you. Couldn't we—once this load's off our minds—all be happy together? (*She looks at David*)

(DAVID, *embarrassed, looks momentarily at Jane, then turns away and moves to* R *of Maureen.* JANE *turns and looks at* VANESSA, *who moves quickly away and sits in the chair down* R)

(*She shakes her head hopelessly*) No, it's no good. (*She moves slowly to the table* C *and picks up her gloves*)

(*The room is deathly still*)

(*She pauses a second, then looks at Bentley. Quietly and unemotionally*) Mr Richmond, I've asked the police to make the fullest investigation into the cause of Richard's death, and to find out if there's any possibility of the existence of poison. (*She picks up the shawl and puts it over the arm holding the gloves, then turns the palms of her hands upwards, looking at them*) And now—if you'll excuse me—I'll—clean—myself.

(JANE *exits slowly up the stairs. The others do not look at her. There is a short silence*)

MAUREEN (*presently; moving above the chair* LC) Father, now don't you see?

(BENTLEY, *not knowing what to think, shakes his head.* DAVID *moves up* RC. VANESSA *rises and crosses to the windows*)

Where are you going, Van?
VANESSA (*pausing*) Into the garden.
BENTLEY (*moving to* L *of Vanessa*) May I come with you?
VANESSA. Yes—I'd like you to.

(BENTLEY *and* VANESSA *exit by the windows*)

DAVID (*moving up* R *of the table* C) I could bite my tongue out.
MAUREEN (*moving to* L *of the chair* C) It was cruel of you, David, horribly cruel.
DAVID. I wasn't thinking! When you've lived so long with a thing, you don't watch every word—every chance remark.
MAUREEN. I wouldn't have called that a chance remark.
DAVID. But it was true. (*He moves below the chair* RC) It *will* be hell till the inquest's over. (*He sits in the chair* RC) But the hell started sooner than I'd bargained for.
MAUREEN (*moving to* L *of David*) It's going to be all right. Your mother'd never be so certain if she'd . . .
DAVID. No—I thought of that. Especially when she asked them to make those tests.
MAUREEN (*moving away up* R) Well, we'll soon know.
DAVID (*rising*) Soon! (*He moves up* R *of the table* C) It'll seem like an age. (*He crosses below the table to* LC) The waiting of years concentrated—compressed—into a week. Look, Maureen—last night I made you promise to marry me whatever happened. I don't know what came over me—I was so scared of losing you I didn't think.

MAUREEN (*moving below the chair* RC) But I did promise, so what's it matter?
DAVID (*moving below the table* C) It's just that I can't drag you into all this.
MAUREEN. Why . . . ?
DAVID (*turning away*) God knows what I'll do without you, but it wouldn't be fair.
MAUREEN (*simply*) And what'll *I* do without you?
DAVID (*sitting on the pouffe and facing* R) Don't make it harder for me, please.
MAUREEN (*kneeling* R *of David; tenderly*) I know what you're feeling—what any man would feel—but why let something outside our control spoil our happiness?
DAVID (*rising*) But that's what I'm trying to make you understand. (*He turns away*) There wouldn't *be* any happiness for you.
MAUREEN. Far more than if we parted.
DAVID. You don't know—I do. (*He sits in the chair* LC) I've lived here in the shadow . . .
MAUREEN (*rising*) We're going away. Where no-one'll know.
DAVID. Your father'll know.
MAUREEN (*moving* LC) I've told him I'll never give you up.
DAVID. He's spoken to you already, has he?
MAUREEN. Yes.
DAVID (*rising and moving to her*) There you are then, you see?
MAUREEN. I've got my own life to live, David. I want to live it with you.
DAVID (*holding her arms*) Yes, but we've not only ourselves to consider, darling—there'll be our children.
MAUREEN. Well?
DAVID. That's what your father's thinking of.
MAUREEN. I'm a doctor, darling. There's nothing to be afraid of.
DAVID. You're sure?
MAUREEN. I want you—I want your children. Would I? If I weren't certain? You must trust me.
DAVID (*crossing below Maureen to* R *of her*) God knows I want to.
MAUREEN. Then it's settled, eh?
DAVID (*turning to her*) If *you're* willing—yes.
MAUREEN (*turning to him and lightly kissing him*) Good. (*She crosses below David to* R) Then you get a special licence and we'll be married as soon as possible.
DAVID. What?
MAUREEN. It'll be easier that way. If we tell him first, Daddy'll only raise a lot of silly objections.
DAVID (*moving to* R *of the table* C) Mother won't be too pleased, either.
MAUREEN. She wouldn't mind so much, if she could go on living here.

DAVID. But I don't see how she can.

MAUREEN. If she wants to, darling, at least give her the chance. (*She sits in the chair* RC) We'll have enough money to get along on.

DAVID (*moving below the chair* C; *dubiously*) I don't know about that.

MAUREEN. It isn't as if I didn't want to go on working. So why not let what I earn make up for what you lose by not selling the house?

DAVID (*sitting in the chair* C) It's sweet of you, but . . .

MAUREEN. Let me do something for your mother, David. When all this trouble's cleared up, I'd like to know things'll be easier for her.

DAVID. You think the trouble *will* be cleared up?

MAUREEN. Of course.

DAVID. Yet you want to get married secretly.

MAUREEN. Only because of daddy. He can be awfully difficult, you know. So—what about it?

DAVID (*rising and moving below the table* C; *smiling*) Well—it's not for me to reason why, I suppose.

MAUREEN (*rising and going to him*) No—nor to look a gift horse in the mouth.

DAVID (*after a pause*) All right.

MAUREEN. I'll make you happy, David.

DAVID (*taking her in his arms*) You've made me happy again already. (*He kisses her*) What I've done to deserve a girl like you, I just don't know.

MAUREEN. And it'd take me far too long to tell you. (*She moves to the foot of the stairs*) I think I'll go and see how your mother is, instead.

DAVID. Don't be long.

(JANE *enters at the top of the stairs*)

MAUREEN (*to Jane*) Oh, I was just coming to see how you were.

JANE (*coming down the stairs*) Better now, thank you, Maureen. (*She crosses to the windows and closes the curtains*) Has your father gone out?

MAUREEN. Just into the garden with Vanessa.

JANE. I must see about supper (*She moves below the table up* LC)

MAUREEN (*moving to* R *of the table up* LC) David and I'll do it. You need to rest.

JANE. Thank you, Maureen. (*She crosses and stands above the chair* C) That's very kind of you.

MAUREEN (*moving to the door down* L) Come on, David.

(DAVID *crosses to Maureen.*
BENTLEY *enters by the windows*)

BENTLEY. I saw you drawing the curtains, ma'am. I hope you're feeling recovered?

ACT II   TELL-TALE MURDER   35

JANE. Yes, thank you. (*She crosses to the dresser and picks up her work-basket*)

MAUREEN. David and I are going to get the supper, Daddy. Are you feeling hungry?

BENTLEY. Take your time as far as I'm concerned.

DAVID. We'll give you a shout when it's ready.

(MAUREEN *and* DAVID *exit down* L)

JANE (*crossing to* R *of the table* C) Well, Mr Richmond, do you still believe I'm guilty?

BENTLEY. I've never said I thought that.

JANE. You didn't need to. Your whole attitude . . .

BENTLEY. Is only what you've made it, Mrs Mannion. (*He moves in slightly*) If what you told me about your mother is true . . .

JANE (*sitting in the chair* C) It was true. (*She puts her work-basket on the table* C)

BENTLEY. But why say such a dangerous thing!

JANE (*taking her sewing from the basket*) She was acquitted, wasn't she? In England you can't be tried twice for the same crime.

BENTLEY (*moving down* LC) Then you must expect me to have misgivings about yourself.

JANE. Of course. You're a lawyer.

BENTLEY (*crossing down* RC) I'm also a father, Mrs Mannion, and that's more important to me at the moment. Please believe that I want you to be innocent, for Maureen's sake. But you must see that, equally for her sake, I've got to prove you guilty if I can.

JANE. Then put me in the witness-box. I *want* to answer your questions.

BENTLEY. Why?

JANE. Because the whole situation's changed. Last night, when I told you about my mother, I didn't know Richard's body would be found. Now, you must hear the rest of the story. So ask your questions. I'll tell you what you want to know. (*She sews*)

BENTLEY. Thank you. (*He paces up* R, *thinking*) Tell me, Mrs Mannion, was your married life happy?

JANE. No.

BENTLEY. There were quarrels?

JANE. Yes.

BENTLEY. Frequent?

JANE. No—but from time to time.

BENTLEY (*moving down* R) Did you love your husband?

JANE. No.

BENTLEY. Were you fond of him?

JANE. In my way—yes.

BENTLEY (*moving down* R *of the table* C) You were, perhaps, grateful to him.

JANE. What for?

BENTLEY. Weren't you a peasant girl? Poor? Because of your mother living under a cloud? He knew about your mother, I suppose?

JANE. Yes.

BENTLEY. Helped her perhaps.

JANE. No. He always refused to meet her—and wouldn't let me have anything to do with her.

BENTLEY (*sitting in the chair* RC) But in spite of all this he married you—gave you a reasonable amount of money—position. He even educated you. Wasn't there cause for gratitude in all that?

JANE. I paid for it. He wanted a housekeeper—*I* was that housekeeper. He wanted a toy to play with—a human toy to mould and re-create. *I* was that toy. But, above all, in the beginning, he wanted me. No, Mr Richmond, there was nothing to be grateful for, believe me. I gave him just as much as he gave me.

BENTLEY. You say in the beginning he wanted you. That didn't last?

JANE. For some years—yes. Then . . .

BENTLEY. Then—you occupied separate rooms.

JANE. Most of the time—yes.

BENTLEY. So though you were fond of your husband, your life with him was neither happy nor normal.

JANE. I can't see it was abnormal. He was seventy, you know.

BENTLEY. And at the time of his—death, we must call it now, mustn't we—you were—how old?

JANE. Thirty-two.

BENTLEY (*rising*) If he'd died a natural death, would you have been sorry?

JANE (*after a slight pause*) No.

BENTLEY. But that didn't stop you taking good care of him.

JANE. No.

BENTLEY (*moving up* R) A man of seventy with indifferent health would need a certain amount of attention—of watchful care—wouldn't he?

JANE. Yes.

BENTLEY (*moving to* R *of the table* C) Then why did you take so long to tell the police he was missing?

(JANE *looks at him*)

I understand there was a lapse of nearly forty-eight hours before you informed them.

JANE (*sullenly*) He'd been missing before.

BENTLEY. So long?

JANE (*grudgingly*) No.

BENTLEY (*moving up* LC) He went out fairly late at night, I'm told, and next morning he hadn't returned.

JANE. He may have.

BENTLEY. And gone out again before you woke up?

JANE. That's what I thought.
BENTLEY (*moving down* LC) His bed—had it been slept in? (*He pauses*) Answer me, Mrs Mannion.
JANE. No.
BENTLEY. Then . . .
JANE. But often he'd work all night—writing—wouldn't go to bed at all.
BENTLEY. I see. (*He moves up* L) So you let that day pass.
JANE. I'm not an alarmist, Mr Richmond.
BENTLEY. But by midnight you had good *cause* for alarm. Surely—by *then* you should have gone to the police?
JANE. We had no phone in those days—it was a pitch black night—and a long, difficult walk to the village.
BENTLEY (*moving towards her; sharply*) A walk you'd done often before.
JANE. Not at night—nor when I was five months gone with child.
BENTLEY (*surprised*) You were . . . ?
JANE. Vanessa was born—prematurely—two months later.
BENTLEY. Couldn't your servant have gone?
JANE (*strongly*) What good would it have done? You can't search for a man in the middle of the night on the Cornish moors.
BENTLEY. If you *wanted* to find him you could try.

(JANE *says nothing, but glooms in her chair*)

(*He moves down* L *of the chair* C) Think of it, Mrs Mannion, in the light of what we now know. (*He crosses to* R *of the table* C) The night before, your husband had fallen down the mineshaft—think of his desperate struggles to get out—think of him tearing at the sides of that shaft to get a foothold—(*he moves up* R) clinging frantically to any ledge—up to his neck in water—his cries for help getting fainter his strength weaker—until at last, in agony and despair, he sinks. (*He moves to* R *of the table and leans across it*) And at the very time when you were saying to yourself I'll wait till morning, there may still have been hope of saving him.
JANE (*turning on him*) But he didn't die like that! He died *quickly*—of a broken neck.
BENTLEY. And if he had to die, shouldn't you be *glad* it was like that? Quickly?
JANE. Yes.
BENTLEY. Yet it seems to be worrying you—this broken neck—to be preying on your mind.
JANE (*her fingers pressing on her temples*) The whole thing's preying on my mind.
BENTLEY. So it should, Mrs Mannion, so it should. However innocent you may be of murder, you're guilty of one thing—criminal delay.

(ELLEN *enters stealthily at the top of the stairs, and stands listening*)

JANE. I know that now.

BENTLEY. Doesn't it look as if you *wanted* some accident to happen to your husband? And did what you could to make that accident fatal?

JANE (*quickly putting her sewing away and rising in an outburst*) You lawyers! (*She picks up her work-basket, crosses to the dresser and puts the basket out of sight in the corner*) You'd twist anything—anything—to make it suit your case.

BENTLEY. I'm trying to get at the truth.

JANE. I'm telling you the truth.

BENTLEY. Then tell me this. Did you want your husband to die?

JANE (*moving up* R *of the chair* RC) Yes.

BENTLEY (*moving up* L *of the chair* RC) And did you—by poison or any other means—bring about his death.

JANE (*moving down* RC) No! I did not.

BENTLEY. Then his death was accidental?

(JANE *shakes her head as if she cannot decide*)

(*He moves above the chair to* R *of Jane*) Come, Mrs Mannion, do you believe his death was accidental?

JANE (*moving above the table* C) I can't say—I can't tell. It may have been.

(ELLEN *exits at the top of the stairs*)

BENTLEY. But it may not have been? Is that what you're trying to imply?

JANE (*banging the back of the chair* C *with her hand*) I don't know, I tell you—I don't know.

BENTLEY. There must be something, Mrs Mannion—something causing these doubts.

JANE (*her mind made up*) Yes. Yes, Mr Richmond, there is. Something that's tortured me far more than anything else in this whole dreadful nightmare.

(ELLEN *enters stealthily at the top of the stairs*)

You asked me if I believed Richard's death was accidental. I don't believe it.

BENTLEY. How *do* you think he died?

JANE. I think—now—what I've sometimes suspected.

BENTLEY. What?

JANE. That my husband *was* murdered.

(ELLEN, *frightened, draws in her breath quickly and quiveringly*. BENTLEY *turns and sees Ellen*)

BENTLEY (*peremptorily*) What are *you* doing there?

JANE. Ellen!
BENTLEY (*moving up* RC) How long have you been listening?

(ELLEN *turns to go*)

JANE. Come back.

(ELLEN *stops and turns*)

(*She moves to the foot of the stairs*) Come down here.

(ELLEN *comes down the stairs*)

BENTLEY. I'm terribly sorry, Mrs Mannion, if she's . . .
JANE. You needn't worry, Mr Richmond. She'd have heard nothing she didn't know already.
BENTLEY. You mean she's . . . ?

(ELLEN, *at the foot of the stairs, looks guiltily at Bentley and Jane*)

JANE (*taking Ellen's arm and leading her* LC) Ellen, I'm telling Mr Richmond all I know about my husband's death. You were here, you know what happened. You can help.
ELLEN. No—no.
JANE (*with underlying menace*) Come and sit down—(*she leads Ellen below the table* C *to the chair* RC) here, and listen.

(ELLEN *sits. She appears to be very nervous*)

(*She moves up* R *of the table* C) So far you've had only my word. Now you can have Ellen to support it.
BENTLEY (*crossing to* LC) I'd rather talk to her afterwards.
JANE. Ellen stays—or I answer no more questions.
BENTLEY. Very well. You were saying, Mrs Mannion, that now you think your husband was murdered. Why?
JANE. Because his neck was broken.

(ELLEN *peers up at Jane in surprise*)

It was always absurd to say I poisoned him. Now, it's more than absurd to say that afterwards I carried his body two miles to the mineshaft to get rid of it.
BENTLEY. I agree, but . . .
JANE (*moving below the table* C) But there's another possibility, Mr Richmond—a possibility I've turned over and over in my mind today till it's become a certainty. Supposing someone followed him that night—(*she moves towards Bentley*) out of this house—across the moor—until, near the mineshaft the opportunity came to . . . (*She turns away above the chair* C) Oh, it's too horrible to think of.
BENTLEY. But you *are* thinking of it, Mrs Mannion.
JANE. I've got to—got to.
BENTLEY. And this *someone*—who was it?
JANE (*moving above the table* C) I can't tell you.

BENTLEY. But you must.

JANE. I'm putting in your mind a possibility. Can't we leave it at that?

BENTLEY. No. It may be established that your husband was indeed murdered. What will your position be then?

JANE (*bitterly*) Worse than it is now?

BENTLEY. Much worse. Everyone points at you now—slanders you without any definite evidence of murder. With murder proved, what will they do then? They'll say it was you—*you, followed him across the moor. You* ...

JANE (*moving down* RC) No! They can't say it. They mustn't.

BENTLEY. Then *who did?*

JANE (*after a pause; trying to control her emotion*) All right, I'll tell you. (*She crosses below Ellen to* R) *We'll* tell you, Ellen and I, what happened that night.

ELLEN. No!

JANE. We've got to, Ellen. You've got to help me. I'll tell what I know—you tell what you told me.

ELLEN. I'm old—I can't remember.

JANE. You must. I wasn't here all the time, was I? You can fill in the gaps. It was you who saw my husband go out, wasn't it, Ellen?

BENTLEY. You mustn't put thoughts into witnesses' minds, Mrs Mannion.

JANE (*flaring at him*) Can I help it with her?

(ELLEN *mutters uneasily*)

(*She crosses above Ellen to* R *of the table* C) She's an old woman, and all this happened a long time ago. I've got to recall it to her.

BENTLEY (*with a slight shrug*) Very well. (*He sits in the chair* LC)

(*There is a slight pause. During Jane's speech the lights fade, almost imperceptibly by stages, until she is left with the light of one spot only on her face*)

JANE. Seeing me as I am now, an ageing, embittered woman, I dare say you'll find it hard to imagine me as I once was—young, happy, and in love. God knows, the happiness didn't last long —two short months, that's all. (*She moves down* C) I'd been married nine years when *he* came, and I fell in love with him. He was a country lad, where from I don't know—a wanderer, tramping from place to place, picking up odd jobs here and there to keep him going. (*She moves up* LC, *looking in the direction of the moor*) Early that spring he pitched his tent out here on the moor. My husband liked him, gave him work, in the garden—around the house. (*She turns to Bentley*) You can probably guess the rest. I was lonely— unhappy—he was young and attractive, and he treated me as a human being. I fell in love with him, and although he was ten years younger—he loved me. You can't know what that meant to me. That summer we lived in a dream. (*She pauses, thinking of it*) Then—everything began to go wrong. (*She moves up* L *of the chair* C, *with her back to Bentley*) He started to make demands on me. (*She moves to the foot of the stairs*) He wasn't satisfied to come here, to this room, in the evenings, unknown to my husband working upstairs. He wanted me to go out to him on the moor at night. But I wouldn't go. (*She moves down a couple of steps*) So he tried threatening me—said he'd tell my husband everything—(*she moves above the table* C) said he'd stop at nothing to get me. (*She faces Bentley*) He'd always hated my husband, now he hated him more than ever because he stood between us. And after two short months of happiness, I was in hell again. (*She is now lit only by the spot*) The strain was telling on me—I was tired, worn out. I couldn't go on as I was. The break had to be made. But which was I to break with? My husband? Or the man I loved?

(*The spotlight starts to fade*)

I had to make up my mind. (*She moves to the foot of the stairs*)

(*The spotlight fades leaving the stage in darkness*)

That night in September I was upstairs, Ellen was down here seeing to the lamps . . .

(*In the* BLACK-OUT JANE *exits up the stairs,* BENTLEY *rises and exits down* L. ELLEN *can be heard crooning wierdly the tune of "Lord Rendel". She rises, moves to the table up* LC, *removes the shade and chimney from the lamp and strikes a match. By its light she can be seen, her back to the audience, lighting the lamp. She adjusts the wick and replaces the chimney and shade. Still crooning, she moves to the foot of the stairs, stops crooning, and listens. Then singing again, she moves to the dresser and repeats the business of lighting the lamp. The room is now comparatively dimly lit, the back wall and stairs being almost in darkness. The furniture is in the same position as before.* ELLEN *looks exactly as she did, but moves more quickly and firmly, speaks with a younger voice, and although still forbidding in demeanour, is far from senile. Her shoulders are straighter and she does not have to peer up at people when talking to them. Having lit the lamp on the dresser,* ELLEN *moves to the cupboard up* R, *opens it, takes a duster and wipes the lamp oil from her fingers. She replaces the duster, closes the cupboard door, and starting to sing again moves up* L. *A low whistle is heard from the garden.* ELLEN *stops, listens, then turns to the stairs and goes up a few steps. She hisses twice, as if to attract someone's attention, and comes downstairs again. There is a pause.*

JANE *enters at the top of the stairs. She has a mass of dark, shoulder-length hair framing her pale face and dark eyes. Her lips are full and red. But she looks strained and tired. She is wearing a full, normal length, dark skirt, and a vivid red woollen jumper with short sleeves and a low, revealing neck*)

(*She leans over the rail*) Is he here?

ELLEN. Outside.
JANE (*glancing at the top of the stairs; doubtfully*) He's still working, but he's so restless—walking up and down—up and down. I don't know if it's . . .

(*The low whistle from the garden is heard again*)

ELLEN (*moving towards the windows*) I'll tell him to be off.
JANE (*coming down several stairs*) No—don't. I've got to see him, but . . . (*She glances off* R) We'll have to risk it. (*She gives a quick nod to Ellen and moves down* R *of the table* C)

(ELLEN *goes to the windows and flicks the centre of the curtains twice, allowing the light inside the room to be seen in the garden*)

Keep watch at the end of the passage.

(ELLEN *moves to the stairs and starts to go up.*

JACK *enters by the windows. The curtains open and close behind him. He stands behind the table up* LC, *the light from the lamp showing him up in relief against the background of the curtains. He is aged about twenty-three, good-looking, of the type so frequently drawn by advertising artists for the lusty young workman. His forehead and eyes are good, his nose and chin well chiselled, his mouth firm, his jaw clean cut, his hair fairish and curly, his shoulders broad, his hips narrow. He is very sun-tanned. He gives the impression of being rather coarse, of the earth, earthy, and very assured, a man who is used to having his own way, especially with women. He is wearing a shirt which is open down to the waist, showing his chest, the sleeves rolled up; dark blue trousers which hang from the hip rather than the waist, kept up by a narrow belt. He holds his position, looking at Jane.* ELLEN *stops and turns.* JACK *smiles, showing good white teeth. Then, jokingly, he puts on the air of an employee before his employer, slightly bends his head, and speaks with a country accent*)

JACK. Good evening, ma'am.
JANE (*turning slightly towards Ellen*) Get upstairs.

(ELLEN *exits up the stairs.* JACK *moves quickly above the table up* LC *to* LC *and holds out his arms.* JANE *crosses to him and they kiss passionately*)

JACK. Three nights I've been waiting for that. I couldn't've waited much longer.
JANE. You've seen me during the day.
JACK. Seeing's fine, but it isn't enough—not for me.
JANE. Nor for me. It's torture having you about all the time and pretending I hardly know you.
JACK. You do hardly know me. But you're going to know me better. (*He kisses her again, at first gently, lingeringly, then suddenly becoming passionate*)

(JANE *struggles a little to release herself, but* JACK *will not let her go until he wishes. Then she pushes him away and moves quickly down RC, and stands with her back to him)*

JANE. No!

(JACK *looks at her, amused and slightly condescending*)

JACK. What's the matter? Afraid?

JANE. Afraid you'll make me forget I'm afraid.

JACK (*moving behind her and putting his hands on her shoulders*) Give me the chance and I'll make you forget everything—except . . .

JANE. What?

JACK (*speaking just behind her ear*) That you're a woman, and— I'm a man. (*His hand goes round her shoulder, then down the side of her breast to her waist*) A man who isn't waiting any longer. When!

JANE (*turning to him*) I don't know.

JACK. Tonight!

JANE (*in sudden panic*) I can't.

JACK. Can't you? (*He takes her in his arms and kisses her*) Now— can't you?

JANE (*breaking from him and crossing to LC*) I must think.

JACK (*crossing to her*) That's it—think. Of the black night and the stars—the wide moor, and a little tent—of me lying there— and you. (*He pauses*) Well?

JANE (*with her back to him*) No.

JACK (*becoming rougher in voice*) You love me, don't you?

JANE. Yes.

JACK. And want me?

JANE. Yes—God help me—I want you.

JACK (*going to embrace her*) Then . . .

JANE (*evading him and moving below the table up LC*) No, Jack. It can't go on—all this.

JACK (*sharply*) What d'you mean?

JANE. Us. We've got to finish.

JACK. Why?

JANE (*glancing at the stairs*) Him.

JACK (*moving quickly to R of her*) What's he matter?

JANE. He's my husband.

JACK (*seizing her fiercely*) He'll never stop me having you. Get that. Not if I have to . . .

JANE (*afraid*) Have to—what?

JACK. I'll show you. (*He whips round to the stairs*)

(JANE *runs after him, desperately turning him on the first stair and clutching his shirt*)

JANE. No, Jack, no, no!

(JACK *seizes her wrists and swings her to R of him*)

JACK. Are you playing some double game with me?

JANE. No.

JACK. Swear!
JANE. I swear it.
JACK. Then we're *not* finishing. You're going to be my woman, husband or no husband. And if it's got to be no husband—it'll *be no husband*.
JANE (*backing from him above the table* C) You don't know what you're saying.
JACK (*moving slowly towards her*) I'm not being put off any longer.
JANE (*almost weeping*) But you don't understand.
JACK. So long as *you* do. (*He moves towards the windows*) I'll be waiting.
JANE (*following him*) Don't go—please don't go.
JACK (*turning*) Well?
JANE. You do believe I want to come, don't you?
JACK (*with a slight return of his former manner*) Sure. And that you'll want to stay.
JANE. Then you *must* believe it's true I can't.
JACK. Look...
JANE. That we've got to say good-bye.
JACK. To hell...
JANE (*almost beside herself*) No, listen, please—listen, listen. (*She moves below the chair* C. *Quickly*) There's something I've hidden from you—something I've known for a long time, but didn't want you to find out.
JACK (*moving* LC) What?
JANE. Something I never dreamed of when you came here—when I fell in love with you.
JACK (*impatiently*) Well, come on. Out with it.
JANE. I'm going to have a child.

(JACK *pauses and clenches his fists. He moves to Jane, seizes her wrists and swings her below him to* L *of him*)

JACK (*furiously*) You told me he never came near you.
JANE. He hasn't—not since...
JACK. Told me you locked your door in case.
JANE. I do.
JACK (*holding her arms*) You're a liar!
JANE (*weeping hysterically*) No!
JACK. Saying you love me one minute, and the next...
JANE. I do love you.

(JACK, *with an exclamation of disbelief, throws her to the floor, so that her fall is broken by the pouffe, and strides away above the chair* LC)

It's five months, Jack, since—since...
JACK. How do I know?
JANE. You can't know—unless you love me—and trust me.
JACK (*after a pause*) All right. I *will* believe you.

JANE (*hopefully*) And you'll go away?
JACK. Oh, no.
JANE. But . . .
JACK (*moving towards her*) I said you were going to be my woman and you're *going* to be my woman. I can wait.
JANE (*rising*) Not here, Jack—you can't stay here.
JACK. I'm staying *right* here. Watching you.
JANE (*slowly*) You can watch, Jack, and you can wait. But you'll have to wait a long time. I've made up my mind, you see. Now this baby's coming I'm going to be a better wife to Richard.
JACK (*menacingly*) You're throwing me over?
JANE. Go away, Jack—miles away. Emigrate, if you like.
JACK. You come with me.
JANE (*moving below the chair* RC) I can't come with you. At least, not until Richard's dead.
JACK (*moving below the table, his gaze fixed towards the top of the stairs*) Not until he's dead.
JANE. Then—if you still want me—I'll marry you.

(ELLEN *enters hastily at the top of the stairs and hisses warningly*)

ELLEN (*coming down the stairs*) He's coming down.
JANE (*to Jack*) Quickly! Through the garden.

(JACK *moves up* LC *then stops and turns.* ELLEN *stands at the foot of the stairs.* JANE *moves quickly to the dresser cupboard, takes a basket of sewing from it, then turns and sees Jack*)

(*She moves to the table* C *and puts the basket on it*) What are you waiting for? He'll . . .
JACK (*stolidly*) I'm not going.
JANE. Don't be a fool!
JACK (*moving menacingly to Jane*) We'll *see* who's the fool.
JANE. Get out—for God's sake.
JACK (*crossing to the cupboard under the stairs*) This may be my chance. (*He opens the cupboard door*)
JANE (*moving to Jack; fearfully*) What're you going to do?
JACK. Wait—(*he backs into the cupboard*) and watch! (*He closes the cupboard door*)

(JANE, *horrified, looks at the cupboard door, then glances quickly upstairs, turns to Ellen and leads her* LC)

JANE (*urgently*) Get out! But stay within call—(*she moves below the table*) for God's sake stay within call.

(ELLEN *crosses and exits down* L. JANE *sits in the chair* C, *takes a piece of embroidery from her basket and sews.*
  RICHARD MANNION *enters at the top of the stairs and comes slowly down. He is a spare man of medium height, looking rather less than his seventy years. His eyes and mouth are cynical; when talking to*

Jane there is the hint of a sneer in his voice. He looks neither ill, nor robust, but carries himself well. He is wearing a suit, old-fashioned in cut, of light texture, and has a signet ring on the little finger of the right hand, the seal of which is plain. He carries a lighted candle in a brass candlestick. He pauses, hand on the newel post, looking at JANE, *who is aware of him standing there, but does not turn or speak*)

RICHARD. What a picture! Penelope waiting the coming of Ulysses. Do you feel like Penelope?
JANE. I don't know who she is.
RICHARD (*crossing to up* L *of Jane and looking down on her*) Ah—no. Penelope was a good Greek housewife. By the way—(*he looks at his hand*) there was no clean towel in the bathroom tonight.
JANE. I'll tell Ellen.
RICHARD (*crossing below the table* C *to* R *of it*) Her husband, Ulysses, left her to go on a voyage of adventure and discovery. (*He puts the candlestick on the table* C) She sat at home, calmly doing her tapestry. Her husband was away so long everyone thought him dead. She had many suitors—but no, you couldn't feel like Penelope—you've never had a suitor.
JANE. Nor is my husband dead.
RICHARD. Time will rectify that, my dear.
JANE. Go on about Penelope.
RICHARD. She loved her husband deeply. Why did I *ever* think you might feel like Penelope? (*He crosses to* L *of Jane*) I must find a legend for you where the wife hated her husband. There are plenty.
JANE (*stopping sewing*) I don't hate you.
RICHARD (*touching her with his left hand*) Then you can't be human. Look at the way I treat you.
JANE (*taking the scissors from her basket*) Need we talk about it?
RICHARD (*moving behind Jane and running his hand slowly over her shoulders and upper arms*) Of course, I've never thought you *were* human—fundamentally. I've probed and goaded you—trying to find your raw spots. You've screamed and spat at me when you've been hurt, yes—but animals do that. I've never yet had a reaction from you that was purely human.

(JANE *drops her scissors on the floor and bends forward to pick them up, thereby avoiding his hands*)

JANE. How's the novel going?
RICHARD. Let's change the subject, eh? That's something I've taught you at least—social adeptness. Though why, God knows! (*He moves up* R *of the table* C) We've no-one to be social with. Not even each other. The novel is not going. I'm stuck, stuck, stuck.
JANE. Have you finished for tonight?
RICHARD. No. It's due at the publishers in a month. I can't afford to miss the spring issues. (*He moves towards the cupboard up* R *and his hand goes out towards the door-knob*)

JANE (*rising convulsively*) What d'you want?
RICHARD (*turning*) My hat.
JANE. You're—going out?
RICHARD. Yes.

(JANE *moves quickly to Richard, trying to speak solicitously, but sounding staccato*)

JANE. Not tonight, Richard, you're tired.
RICHARD. This solicitude's a little sudden, isn't it?
JANE (*leading him to the chair* RC) Sit down for a while—rest.
RICHARD. Is this a trick?
JANE. No.
RICHARD. Then . . .

(JANE *gently sits* RICHARD *in the chair* RC *and pushes his head back till it rests on the back of the chair*)

JANE. Don't try to talk. Lie your head back—relax. Close your eyes, and rest.

(RICHARD *closes his eyes.* JANE, *with her hand on Richard's forehead, turns her head slowly and looks apprehensively over her shoulder at the cupboard door*)

Have your warm milk now. It might make you sleep for a while. Then you'll work all the better.
RICHARD (*wearily*) I am tired.
JANE (*very quietly*) Ssh! (*She crosses noiselessly towards the door down* L)

(*The cupboard door opens slowly and* JACK *comes out. In his hand he holds a woman's red silk scarf. He stands quite silently and winds either end of the scarf round each hand, and draws the scarf taut. Silently he moves carefully down behind Richard's chair*)

(*She opens the door down* L *and calls softly*) Ellen! Ellen! (*She holds the door open, waiting for Ellen, then turns in time to see Jack*)

(JACK, *standing behind Richard, slowly raises his hands, the scarf tightly stretched between them.* JANE'S *hand goes to her mouth and she draws in her breath with terror, making a strangled sound. She must not scream.* RICHARD *opens his eyes and sits up.*

ELLEN *enters down* L. JACK *releases the scarf from one hand and plunges the other with the scarf into his trouser pocket and moves to* R *of Richard*)

RICHARD. What's the matter? (*His eyes following Jane's, he turns and sees Jack*) What're you doing here?
JACK. Waiting to see you.
RICHARD. Why? (*He sees the open cupboard door, then turns to look at Jane*) What's going on?
JANE. Warm the master's milk for him, Ellen.

(ELLEN *exits down* L. JANE *closes the door*)

RICHARD. Well?
JANE (*moving* LC) Jack wanted to see you.
RICHARD. So he said. Did you think I was in that cupboard?
JACK. You and me's got to have a talk.
RICHARD. What about?
JACK (*looking at Jane*) Her.
JANE. Not now, Jack.
JACK. Now.
RICHARD (*looking at them; a cynical twist to his mouth*) You don't mean . . .
JACK. She's finished with you——
JANE. No.
JACK. —leaving you. And coming to me.
RICHARD (*his amusement growing slightly*) You and she are . . . ?
JACK. Lovers.
JANE. I asked you not to . . .

(JANE *breaks off as* RICHARD *begins to laugh, quietly at first, then with less restraint.* JACK *looks at him in amazement, then makes a move as if to attack him*)

JACK. What the . . .
JANE (*with a step forward*) No, Jack!
RICHARD. You poor fool! You don't really think she'd go away with you, do you?
JACK. Why not?
RICHARD. You don't *know* Jane. She realizes when she's well off. She's like a cat—a sulky cat, perhaps——

(JANE *moves slowly* LC)

—but still a cat. She never purrs, but she likes the best place on the hearthrug, the warmest spot near the fire. Try to move her from 'em, and you'll see some claws.
JANE (*turning fiercely on him*) You . . .
RICHARD. She's just been playing with you.

(JACK *moves slowly across to Jane*)

You're her little mouse—her poor little goldfish in a bowl.
JACK (*to Jane*) Is that true?
JANE. No. (*She points at Richard*) He's the one that's playing. You must have heard what he said just now—how he's always goading me—getting at me—forcing me to react as he calls it. (*She moves below the table* C) That's what he's doing now. Just to see what we'll do.
JACK (*loweringly*) He'll see what I'll do. (*He moves towards Richard*)
JANE (*restraining him*) Jack!

RICHARD (*rising; contemptuously*) I'll see you get out of here—now. Pack up your things and clear. She's my wife, and she's staying my wife. Even after I'm dead, she'll *still* be my wife. I'll arrange my affairs in such a way, by God, no-one else'll want her. Now—get out. (*He moves down R and stands with his back to them, playing with the ring on his finger*)
JANE. Please, Jack, it's better.
JACK. You won't come with me?
JANE. I've told you—I can't.
JACK. Not until . . .
RICHARD (*turning*) Until when?
JACK. The morning—maybe.

(JACK *turns and exits quickly by the windows.* JANE *follows him to* LC *and stands looking after him.* RICHARD *stares cruelly at Jane for a moment*)

RICHARD (*crossing to R of Jane; silkily*) So—she got herself a lover, did she? A fine, handsome, sweaty clod of a lover.
JANE (*sullenly*) He's worth ten of you.
RICHARD. Physically, I've no doubt. (*He puts his hand on her shoulder, slowly moving it down her arm*) And you've let those rough hands paw you, have you? Those brutish lips kiss you, have you? P'raps you've even . . . (*He seizes her wrist and turns her to him. Suddenly and violently*) Have you?
JANE (*looking full at him and almost shouting her defiance*) Suppose I have!

(RICHARD, *with an exclamation, throws Jane to the floor by the pouffe.* JANE *weeps.* RICHARD *crosses to the cupboard under the stairs and takes out a long thin leather strap. He moves down* RC *and stands looking at* JANE, *who, seeing the strap, stops weeping, rises and backs* LC)

RICHARD. Get to your room.

(ELLEN *enters down* L *and stands in the doorway. She carries a glass of milk on a small tray*)

JANE (*her eyes on the strap; in a low voice*) You're not going to . . . ?
RICHARD. Not tonight. You can spend tonight thinking about it. And in the morning . . . (*He runs his hand lovingly along the strap*)

(JANE, *sobbing, goes quickly to the stairs and pauses at the newel post*)

Good night, my dear.

(JANE *runs up the stairs and exits*)

(*He puts the strap on the table* C *and turns to Ellen*) What d'you want?
ELLEN (*crossing to* LC) Your milk.

RICHARD (*moving to Ellen and taking the glass*) Ah, yes, my milk. (*He sits in the chair* C *and sips the milk*)

(ELLEN *moves above the table* C, *puts the tray on it; then picks up the sewing basket and moves towards the dresser*)

Did *you* know about this?

ELLEN (*pausing*) What?

RICHARD. Your mistress and this gardener fellow.

ELLEN (*putting the basket in the dresser cupboard*) What about them?

RICHARD. So you *did* know.

ELLEN (*turning*) I . . .

RICHARD. Don't protest. I ask you a question in such a way you can't misunderstand, and you *pretend* you don't know what I mean. Which shows you did know. (*He sips his milk*)

(ELLEN *moves to* R *of the table* C)

In the morning, Ellen, that man is going. You'll be going, too.

ELLEN (*unemotionally*) Where *can* I go?

RICHARD. Where did you come from? Only you and your mistress know. Go back there.

ELLEN. I can't. I'm old. No-one'll want me anywhere else.

RICHARD. Nobody wants you here.

ELLEN. *She* does.

RICHARD. That's of small importance. See you're gone before she's up.

ELLEN. Can't I . . . ?

RICHARD (*rising and putting the empty glass on the tray*) That milk wasn't sweet enough. (*He picks up the strap, moves to the cupboard, puts the strap inside, and closes the door*)

(ELLEN *picks up the tray, crosses to the dresser and puts the tray and glass on it, out of sight*)

If you'd been staying, I'd have told you to put more sugar in next time. As it is, I'll have to tell my—loving wife. (*He crosses to the windows*) Put out the lamps, but leave the windows open. I'm going out for a while. Wish me good night, Ellen.

ELLEN (*over her shoulder*) Good night.

RICHARD (*with a cruel smile*) I shan't be seeing you again, shall I?

(RICHARD *looks at Ellen for a moment, the smile still on his lips, then turns and exits by the windows.* ELLEN *moves swiftly above the table* C, *looking after him. When the curtains have closed behind him, she seizes the candle from the table* C, *holds it above her head and speaks in a low voice full of hatred*)

ELLEN. May God's curse and the devil's curse fall on him this night. (*She blows out the candle to complete the curse*)

(*The lights dim quickly to* BLACK-OUT. *In the* BLACK-OUT, ELLEN *puts the candlestick with the others on the chest, then gives a little senile chuckle and can be heard talking as she moves to the chair* RC *and sits. While she talks,* JANE *enters down the stairs and stands up* L *of Ellen, and puts her hand on Ellen's shoulder.* BENTLEY *enters down* L *and sits in the chair* LC.)

(*During the* BLACK-OUT) I cursed him that night. Hey! Who'd a' thought—*you* wouldn't 'a thought, would you, Mr—er—(*she mutters in an attempt to remember the name*) er—Richmond, an old beldam's curse would 'a done what mine did. (*She chuckles again, then turns serious*) He was a black 'un, Richard Mannion, treatin' . . .
    JANE (*sharply*) Ellen!

(*The lights come slowly up until the room is lit as it was before the story started. The dialogue continues all the time.*)

ELLEN (*turning to Jane*) Ummm?
JANE. It's time you were in bed.
ELLEN (*touchily*) Leave me alone. I—I'm enjoying myself. (*She sinks back in her chair*) Eh, dear me, it was a long time ago. (*Plaintively*) How long ago was it?
JANE. Seventeen years.
ELLEN (*meditatively*) H'mmm.

(*By now the lights are full up. The room is exactly as it was.* ELLEN *is seated* RC, *huddled in the chair, a senile smile on her face. Her mouth has been dribbling.* JANE *is standing* L *of Ellen.* BENTLEY *is seated* LC.)

(*She shakes her head. Puzzled*) What was I saying? I forget. I'm old—I—(*her voice fades*) forget.
    BENTLEY (*rising*) So—(*he moves up* L *of the chair* C) in the morning your husband's missing, and knowing what happened the night before, did you go out to the tent on the moor?
    JANE. Yes.
    BENTLEY. And . . . ?
    JANE. It was gone.
    BENTLEY. Your lover, too?
    JANE (*turning away to* L *of chair* RC) Yes.
    BENTLEY (*moving up* LC *towards the table; casually*) When did your lover come back?
    JANE. Come back?
    BENTLEY. He did come back, didn't he?

(JANE *does not know how to answer. Her eyes meet Ellen's.* ELLEN *gives an almost imperceptible nod*)

JANE. Oh, yes. (*She moves above the table* C) Some—time—later.
    BENTLEY (*moving to the chair* LC) It would have been strange if he hadn't, wouldn't it?
    JANE. Yes.

BENTLEY (*sitting* LC) His only reason for doing—what he might have done—was to get you. What happened?
JANE. I sent him away again.
BENTLEY. Why?
JANE (*moving to* L *of the chair* C) How could I have anything more to do with him after what I'd seen?
BENTLEY. You loved him.
JANE. Yes—but . . .
BENTLEY. You loved your mother—and lived with her.
JANE. My mother risked her life for *me*.
BENTLEY. Hadn't Jack?
JANE. No.
BENTLEY (*incredulously*) No?
JANE. At least, so he said.
BENTLEY (*exasperated*) I don't understand. First you say one thing—then another.
JANE. Because that's how I've thought. First one thing, then another. When he came back he didn't know about Richard—or *said* he didn't. I wanted so desperately to believe him, I *did* believe him—until . . .
BENTLEY. Well? When?
JANE. A few hours ago—when they told me about—the broken neck. Then I saw the scarf—the red scarf—tightly stretched—slowly rising—and I knew—I *knew*—Richard had been murdered.
BENTLEY. What became of the man whose hands held that scarf?
JANE. Mmm?
BENTLEY. What became of your lover?
JANE. I don't know. He just went. (*She moves down* L *of the table* C) I've never seen him again.
BENTLEY. H'mmm. Well—it's a complicated story.
JANE (*making a statement*) You don't believe it.
BENTLEY (*rising*) Mrs Mannion, I don't know *what* to believe.

(JANE *makes a hopeless gesture and sits in the chair* C, *facing Bentley*)

(*He moves up* LC) You and your housekeeper have told me a story so detailed I think much of it *must* have happened. But whether it happened on the night in question—or on any one single night, I just don't know. (*He moves up* R) It may be a hotch-potch—a hotch-potch of incidents—(*he moves to* R *of the table* C) which you've woven and embroidered into a pattern—a pattern whose central figure's only too well known to the criminal courts.
JANE. But . . .
BENTLEY (*crossing below the table to* LC) The man who *comes* from the Unknown—vanishes *back* to the Unknown. The man who committed the crime. Mr X. Mrs Mannion. That's what we

call him—Mr X. And any lawyer can turn him into Mr Why. *Why* can't he be found? *Why* should the Court believe even in his *existence?* You, Mrs Mannion, tell me this story, but can you *prove* it?

JANE (*hopelessly*) No.

BENTLEY. Then I—standing for the Court—must say there never *was* such a man.

JANE (*rising and facing him*) There was! There was.

BENTLEY (*overriding her*) That he doesn't *exist*, Mrs Mannion, and *never did*. (*He turns away to* R *of the table up* LC)

JANE (*with a faltering step towards him*) But . . .

MAUREEN (*off down* L; *calling*) All right—I'll tell them.

(JANE *moves above the table* C. DAVID *and* MAUREEN *enter down* L)

Supper's all ready.

JANE. Thank you.

DAVID (*crossing towards the chest*) Would anyone like a drink first? (*He pauses and looks at Ellen*) Hello—what's . . . ?

JANE (*moving to* L *of Ellen*) Mr Richmond's been talking to Ellen.

DAVID. Oh. (*He crosses to the chest and pours two drinks*)

JANE. Thank you, Ellen, you were very helpful. (*She moves to the chest and lights a candle*) I'll see you to your room.

ELLEN (*levering herself out of the chair*) I can manage—I can manage. (*She moves below the table* C *to* L *of the chair* C)

MAUREEN (*moving to Ellen*) Are you better now?

(JANE, *carrying the lighted candle, moves to the stairs and stands waiting*)

ELLEN. Better?

MAUREEN. Yes. What was wrong?

ELLEN. Oh—(*she maunders*) nothing—(*she moves to the stairs*) nothing.

(MAUREEN *crosses to* R *of the table* C)

Better now—better now.

(JANE *bends to take Ellen's arm. But* ELLEN *snatches the candle, turns and looks at* BENTLEY, *who stares at her, remembering her curse*)

JANE (*sharply*) Come, Ellen.

(JANE *exits up the stairs*.

ELLEN, *whimpering and muttering, follows Jane off.* DAVID *picks up a glass of whisky and turns towards Bentley*)

MAUREEN. What's been happening, Daddy?

BENTLEY (*crossing to David*) Mrs Mannion and I have been getting better acquainted. (*He takes the glass*) Thank you, David.

MAUREEN. But . . .

(VANESSA *enters by the windows and moves below the table up* LC. BENTLEY, *seeing Vanessa, moves to Maureen and puts his hand warningly on her arm*)

BENTLEY (*to Maureen; very quietly*) Ssh! (*He moves to* R *of the chair* RC)

MAUREEN. Hello, Van. (*She crosses to* LC) Where've *you* been all this time?

(DAVID *picks up his own drink*)

VANESSA. On the moor. Your car's outside, Mr Richmond. I've been talking to your chauffeur.

BENTLEY. I'd better go and see him. (*He drinks*)

VANESSA. There's no hurry. I've asked him if he'd like a drink. (*She crosses to* L *of David*) What'll I take him?

DAVID. Why not bring him in?

BENTLEY. But . . .

MAUREEN (*moving to the windows*) I'll go, I haven't seen him yet.

(MAUREEN *exits by the windows*)

BENTLEY. No—Maureen! (*But Maureen has gone. To David*) Your mother mightn't . . .

DAVID. She won't mind.

(BENTLEY *takes a drink from his glass, then puts it on the dresser*)

VANESSA. How is mother, David?

DAVID (*uneasily*) All right.

VANESSA. I hurt her, I know.

(JANE *enters on the stairs and comes slowly down*)

(*She moves up* L *of the table* C) But I couldn't help it.

JANE (*on the stairs*) Well, Vanessa?

VANESSA (*turning swiftly to face Jane; faintly*) Hello, Mother.

JANE (*coming down the stairs and crossing up* LC) I'm glad you're back.

(VANESSA *moves to* R *of Jane*)

I don't like you being out on the moors so late. (*She puts her hand affectionately on Vanessa's shoulder*) What have you told the stars tonight?

VANESSA. Nothing, Mother.

JANE. Wise child. They know it already. (*She crosses down* RC)

(BENTLEY *moves to* R *of Jane.* VANESSA *moves to the foot of the stairs*)

I'm sorry to keep you waiting, Mr Richmond . . .

MAUREEN (*off*) Come along, don't be shy.

(MAUREEN *enters by the windows. Behind her,* HOWELL's *hand holds the curtains apart, although he is not seen*)

(*She moves up* LC) Oh, Mrs Mannion——

(HOWELL *enters by the windows*)

—this is our chauffeur, John Howell.

(HOWELL *takes off his peaked cap with his left hand, which obscures his face. The curtains fall behind him. He stands behind the table up* LC, *the light from the lamp shining on him, framing him against the background of the curtains. He lowers his hand and holds his cap with both hands. He is "Jack" of Jane's story. His face is only older because it is more set and serious, but his curly hair is well-brushed and controlled. He wears a dark blue chauffeur's uniform, the jacket of which buttons across on to the right shoulder, with a high collar, showing no shirt.* JANE *turns away from Bentley and starts to move forward, but seeing Howell, she stops dead*)

HOWELL (*without his country accent*) Good evening, ma'am.

(JANE *sways slightly and tries to speak*)

JANE. Good . . . (*She tries to control herself, but fails*) Good . . . (*She suddenly slumps to the floor above the pouffe, in a faint*)

DAVID *and* MAUREEN *run to* JANE. HOWELL *stays where he is.* BENTLEY *and* VANESSA *stare at Howell as—*

the CURTAIN *falls*

ACT III

Scene I

Scene—*The same. Midday, the following day.*

When the Curtain *rises the room is empty. Although it is a fine day the room is shady and cool, as the sun has not got round to this side of the house.* Vanessa *enters immediately and runs down the stairs to the open windows. She wears a light summer frock.*

Vanessa (*pausing in the windows and calling*) Mr Howell!

(Vanessa *exits by the windows*)

(*Off; calling*) Mr Howell!

(After a pause the voices of Vanessa *and* Howell *are heard off approaching the windows)*

(*Off*) No, please do, I'm all alone. I want to talk to you.
Howell (*off*) Can't we talk out here?
Vanessa (*off*) It's too hot—there's no shade anywhere.

(Vanessa *enters by the windows*)

(*Over her shoulder*) You must be boiling in those clothes. (*She moves up* LC)

(Howell *enters by the windows. He is dressed the same as the previous evening, but has left his cap in the car. He is a very different type of man from the picture drawn by Jane. He is quiet and unassuming, with a slow smile, and a very definite charm. It is evident he has taken a liking to* Vanessa, *as she has to him*)

Howell (*moving to* L *of Vanessa*) I'm used to it hotter than this, miss.
Vanessa. I saw you drive up from my window.
Howell. Mr Richmond wanted me here by twelve-thirty.
Vanessa. He went out—oh, very early—but he knows lunch is at one, so he won't be long.
Howell. That's fine.

(*There is a slight pause.* Vanessa *smiles shyly at* Howell, *who returns the smile*)

Vanessa. Do sit down.
Howell (*uneasily*) I don't think I'd better, miss.
Vanessa. Not just for a minute?
Howell. Well—just for a minute.

VANESSA (*indicating the chair* LC) Here?
HOWELL (*sitting in the chair* LC) Thank you. How is—your mother?
VANESSA. All right now. It was just the strain of all she'd been through. David's taken her to St Ives for the—the inquest.
HOWELL (*uncomfortably*) Oh.
VANESSA. You've heard all about it, I suppose?
HOWELL. Yes.
VANESSA. It's—(*she turns away slightly*) very upsetting—for all of us.
HOWELL. Do *you* remember your father?
VANESSA (*moving down* C) No. I was born after—after it happened. (*She sits on the pouffe and faces Howell*) I've often wondered about him, though—what it would have been like if he'd come back. Sometimes I've sort of—dreamed about him—made up stories to myself of what we might have done together—the happy times we'd have had.
HOWELL. I'm sure you would've.
VANESSA. Fathers're funny creatures. You read about them deserting their wives and children—never caring if they see them again or not. Can you imagine how a man could *do* that?

(HOWELL *does not reply. He is sitting rather tensely*)

Can you?
HOWELL. No.
VANESSA. If I had a baby, I'd want to be with it all the time—watching it grow up, protecting it from any harm. I don't know how anybody could be so *cruel* as to go away and *forget* they have a child. (*She looks at him a little more closely*) You know—you *are* feeling the heat—your forehead's all perspiry. (*She rises*) I'll get you a drink.
HOWELL (*half rising*) I should be . . .
VANESSA. Please stay—it's lonely here. And, after all, you didn't have the one I promised you last night.

(HOWELL *resumes his seat*)

(*She moves towards the chest*) What would you like? Sherry? Whisky? (*She turns and moves* LC) Or would you rather have beer?
HOWELL. I would rather, yes, miss.
VANESSA (*crossing quickly to the door down* L) I'll get you some.
HOWELL (*rising hastily*) No, please don't bother.
VANESSA (*opening the door and calling*) Ellen!

(VANESSA *exits down* L)

HOWELL (*startled*) Ellen!
VANESSA (*off; calling*) Ellen!

(HOWELL *gives a quick, worried look towards the door, then moves down* R *of the table* C *and wipes his brow with his handkerchief.*

(VANESSA *enters down* L *and crosses to* L *of the chair* C)

She's bringing it.

HOWELL. You shouldn't have troubled, miss.

VANESSA. It's no trouble. It's nice to have someone to talk to, and—(*she smiles shyly*) I like you.

HOWELL (*smiling at her*) I'm glad.

(*The door down* L *opens.* HOWELL *looks quickly at the door, then moves down* R *and stands slightly averted.*

ELLEN *shuffles in down* L, *carrying a small tray with an opened bottle of beer and a glass. Her head is bent, intent on the tray she holds.* HOWELL *watches her, tense, waiting for the recognition.* VANESSA *moves above the table* C. ELLEN *crosses to the table* C *and puts the bottle and glass on it. As she straightens,* HOWELL *turns to her. She looks directly at him under her brows. He braces himself and returns her look.*

ELLEN *slowly turns away, drops her head, and shuffles off with the tray down* L. HOWELL *relaxes.* VANESSA *picks up the bottle and glass and pours the beer*)

VANESSA. I'll pour it for you. I do it for David, sometimes.

HOWELL. I dare say you'll miss him when he gets married.

VANESSA. Yes. I try not to think about it. (*She puts the bottle on the table*) There! (*She moves to Howell and hands him the beer*)

HOWELL (*raising the glass*) Happier days, miss. (*He drinks*)

VANESSA (*simply*) Thank you.

HOWELL. That's better.

VANESSA. Good?

HOWELL. Very good.

VANESSA (*sitting curled up in the chair* RC) You're English, aren't you?

HOWELL. Yes. I emigrated—(*he checks himself and moves* R) ooh, nearly twenty years ago.

VANESSA. And have you got relations here? Father? Mother?

HOWELL. No, miss, I've no-one.

VANESSA. Not in South Africa?

HOWELL. No.

VANESSA. You must feel lonely, sometimes, too.

HOWELL. Now and again. But Mr Richmond's very good to me.

VANESSA. He asked me this morning if I'd like to go to South Africa—just for a holiday, of course.

HOWELL (*pleased*) Did he?

VANESSA. But—(*she half turns away from him*) mother'd never let me go.

HOWELL. Don't give up hope. (*He moves to the table* C) Something *might* happen to make her change her mind.

VANESSA (*rising*) You don't mean—anything to do with the inquest?

HOWELL. No, I wasn't thinking of that. (*Pondering, he puts his half-finished glass of beer on the table* C) But it *could* make a difference, of course.

(BENTLEY *enters by the windows. He carries his hat*)

BENTLEY. Hello, John, you're here.
HOWELL. Yes, sir. The young lady asked me in for a drink.
BENTLEY (*moving* LC) That was very kind of you, Vanessa.
HOWELL. I'll wait in the car, sir.
BENTLEY (*moving below the table* C) No, no, finish your drink. I want to have a word with you.

(HOWELL *picks up his glass and moves above the chair* C)

VANESSA. Is there any news—about the inquest?
BENTLEY. No, my dear, it's bound to be adjourned.
VANESSA. Oh.
BENTLEY (*putting his hand on her shoulder*) Don't worry.
VANESSA (*looking down*) It's not very easy.
BENTLEY. I know.
VANESSA (*turning abruptly*) I'll go and give Ellen a hand with the lunch. (*She crosses to the door down* L)

(BENTLEY *turns and looks after her*)

(*She stops* LC *and turns*) I'll see you again, won't I, Mr Howell?
HOWELL. Yes, miss. (*He indicates the beer*) And, thank you.

(VANESSA *smiles at Howell and exits down* L)

BENTLEY. I'm sorry for that child.
HOWELL. Yes, sir.
BENTLEY (*moving to the cupboard up* R *and putting his hat in it*) I wish I could be sure what life's got in store for her.
HOWELL. Couldn't you help in any way, sir?
BENTLEY. I don't know, John, I don't know. (*He moves to the dresser*) In a way, I suppose, it all depends . . . (*He leaves the sentence in mid-air*)
HOWELL (*after a pause*) Yes, sir?
BENTLEY (*turning and looking reflectively at Howell*) To a very great extent on you.
HOWELL (*after a short pause*) I don't get what you mean, sir.

(BENTLEY *snaps out of his reflective mood, moves to the chair* RC *and sits*)

BENTLEY. John, I've been walking this morning and I've walked a long way. Amongst other places I visited the village. I wanted to talk to you.
HOWELL (*moving down* LC) I'm sorry, sir, but you did say twelve-thirty here, and I went to St Ives for petrol.
BENTLEY. So they told me. You know Cornwall quite well, don't you, John?

HOWELL. Fairly, sir.

BENTLEY. I remember your saying so when Maureen came here. And later, when she got engaged, the name Mannion seemed to strike a chord with you.

HOWELL (*putting his glass on the table* C) Yes—but it's a common name hereabouts.

BENTLEY. Why d'you tell me that?

HOWELL (*slightly confused*) Well, sir—I thought perhaps—well, that you might be thinking . . . (*He breaks off*)

BENTLEY (*looking keenly at him*) Thinking what?

HOWELL (*struggling to get out of his difficulty*) Well—that—that I'd heard of this Mannion mystery before.

BENTLEY. And you haven't?

HOWELL. No, sir. It was after my time.

BENTLEY (*nodding towards the chair* LC) Sit down.

HOWELL (*looking uncomfortably at the door down* L) But . . .

BENTLEY. Do as you're told, John.

(HOWELL *sits in the chair* LC)

(*He rises, moves to the table* C *and pours more beer into Howell's glass*) In my profession I've learnt that coincidences, almost incredible coincidences, happen more often than's generally believed. As a lawyer, I deal with *situations*, many of them *created* only by coincidence. So I have to believe these coincidences do happen. (*He moves to Howell and gives him the glass of beer*) Without them there wouldn't *be* a situation—the case would never come to court.

HOWELL (*taking the glass*) Thank you, sir.

BENTLEY (*moving to the chest and putting the beer bottle on it out of sight*) Last night, John, a situation was created here in this room. Mrs Mannion, a strong-minded woman—(*he moves to* R *of the table* C) well in control, I should have thought, of any situation, however abnormal, faints at the very moment she sees you for the first time. Extraordinary, wasn't it?

HOWELL. Yes, sir. (*He raises his glass to drink*)

BENTLEY (*looking piercingly at him*) Was it the first time?

HOWELL (*lowering his glass untasted*) You think . . .

BENTLEY (*disregarding him and moving* LC) Mrs Mannion's told me a great many things since I came here, John—a great many. Amongst others—(*he watches Howell closely*) that she had a lover.

(HOWELL *sits perfectly still, gripping his glass*)

A young man who worked here at "Porthenis". I'm making a long shot, John, acting on a hunch, but—were *you* Jane Mannion's lover?

HOWELL (*unemotionally*) No, sir.

BENTLEY. I'm not taking that for an answer.

HOWELL (*half rising*) But . . .

BENTLEY (*ignoring him*) Think—and then tell me again. (*He

Scene I   TELL-TALE MURDER   61

moves up L *of the chair* C) I am certain Mrs Mannion murdered her husband——

(HOWELL *looks quickly at Bentley*)

—or was implicated in his murder. If, actually, you *were* her lover, and persist in denying it, you must have some reason—ten to one a guilty reason. Now—were you her lover?

HOWELL (*after a short pause*) No, sir.

BENTLEY. H'mm (*He moves up* LC. *More to himself than to Howell*) It's generally assumed, you know, that Richard Mannion was poisoned. In which case he probably died in this house. This morning I walked to that mineshaft where his body was found. Just on two miles—in some places a difficult climb.

(HOWELL, *very uneasy, rises, moves to the table* C *and puts his glass on it*)

If Mrs Mannion poisoned her husband—if he died in this house—the body got from here to there. How? That's what I want to know—*how?* She couldn't have carried it by herself. She must have had an accomplice.

HOWELL. Ellen?

BENTLEY (*turning quickly*) What do *you* know about Ellen?

HOWELL (*taken aback*) Nothing.

BENTLEY (*moving down* L *of the chair* C) Have you met her?

HOWELL. She brought the beer.

BENTLEY. What makes you think *she's* in this?

HOWELL. I . . .

BENTLEY. You don't even know she was here at the time.

HOWELL. But . . .

BENTLEY. You're a rotten liar, John Howell. Whatever else you may be, you're a poor liar. You *know* Ellen was here, because you were here yourself.

HOWELL (*with bent head*) Yes, sir.

BENTLEY (*more kindly*) Better tell me the rest.

HOWELL (*turning away to* R *of the chair* RC) Not now, sir, please.

BENTLEY. Now, John.

HOWELL. You don't know what you're asking me to do.

BENTLEY. I'm asking you to help me, John. To help Maureen.

HOWELL. I can't!

BENTLEY. But *you* know. *You know* what happened to Richard Mannion.

HOWELL. No.

BENTLEY. Then at least you were the last man to see him alive.

HOWELL (*surprised*) *I* was?

BENTLEY. According to Mrs Mannion.

HOWELL (*moving below the chair* RC) My last night here was the night he . . . ?

BENTLEY. The night he died—yes.

HOWELL (*sitting in the chair* RC) God!
BENTLEY. You see how near it's getting to you?
HOWELL. You don't suspect—*I*—had something to do with it?
BENTLEY. *You* tell *me* how *you* think he died.
HOWELL (*tense but reluctant*) I think—the same as you, sir. That she—poisoned him.
BENTLEY. Why do you think that?

(HOWELL *shakes his head*)

(*He moves up* L *of the chair* RC) Tell me—very quietly. No need to hurry. (*He pauses*)

(HOWELL *is silent*)

(*He moves above Howell to* R *of him. Prompting sympathetically*) You came here in the spring, didn't you? You pitched your tent on the moor—Richard Mannion gave you work. Were you happy?
HOWELL (*quietly and slowly*) To begin with—yes. Mannion was a peculiar man—I didn't take to him. But he treated me all right.
BENTLEY. And—Mrs Mannion?
HOWELL. I liked. I didn't know much about—well—anything in those days. I'd lived alone since I was fifteen—never staying in one place long—always avoiding being too near houses and people. They rather frightened me. So though I was twenty-three I'd no experience of women.
BENTLEY (*crossing slowly to the chair* LC) What happened?
HOWELL. I'd only been here two or three days when she began to tell me how unhappy she was—how hardly he treated her. She even showed me a strap and said he beat her with it. I didn't believe her, and she knew it.

(BENTLEY *sits in the chair* LC)

But one night—I was half asleep—she came to the tent and showed me. I saw the weals on her back—across her thighs. I saw a naked woman for the first time, and—(*he drops his head and speaks very low*) I wanted her. But still nothing would have happened if she hadn't shown quite so plainly she wanted me. She was a very passionate woman. I didn't know—I thought all women must be like that—but it revolted me. (*He rises and moves up* L *of the chair* RC) And yet—to begin with, night after night I couldn't rest until she came to me. Sometimes I'd go up to the house of an evening and sit with her—we arranged signals to show if it was safe. But I was never comfortable—with him hidden away working—and Ellen keeping watch. How they both hated him! (*He moves up* R *of the table* C) Then, as the weeks went by, he began to get ill. I'd never seen such a change in a man—it didn't seem natural. I started to wonder. Already I wasn't as keen as I had been, and the more I showed it, the more she demanded of me. I knew at the back of my mind it must end soon. (*He picks up his glass from the table and moves to* L *of the chair* C) That last night—the night you say he died—I came here because Mannion had sent for me—something he'd never done before. I wasn't sure if he might have found out.

(*The lights begin to fade*)

It was a dark night—(*he moves to the windows*) and very quietly I crept up to the windows here, hoping I might get some line as to what was going on. I listened, but heard nothing.

(*The lights* BLACK-OUT)

Then—very carefully—I looked through the windows. Ellen was alone in the room . . .

(*In the* BLACK-OUT, HOWELL *exits by the windows.* BENTLEY *exits down* L. ELLEN, *carrying her properties, enters down the stairs, moves above the table* C, *and puts the properties on it. She can be heard muttering, but the muttering is not senile, more like an incantation.*
The lights come slowly up. It is night, and the room is approximately as it was for the previous flashback, except that the window curtains are open, and only the lamp on the dresser is lit, leaving the left side of the room in comparative darkness. ELLEN *is standing above the table* C. *In the middle of the table is a rough clay or waxen figure of a man, about nine inches high. Beside it is a hatpin about four inches long.* ELLEN *is muttering her spell to the image. She stops muttering, dives into her apron pocket and fishes out the withered, mummified hand of a child, severed at the wrist, lays it on the table pointing at the image. With her finger she draws an imaginary circle on the top of the table round the object, then she picks up the pin, draws her thumb and finger along its length and feels the point with the tip of her finger.*
JANE *enters at the top of the stairs, and pauses a moment. She is dressed as in the previous flash-back, but no longer looks tired. There is a triumphant glow about her, and she gives the same impression as a luscious, ripe fruit. She watches Ellen over the rail of the stairs.* ELLEN *mutters momentarily over the pin, then bending over the table she picks up the image*)

ELLEN. 'Tis not your heart that I would pierce, but the heart of Richard Mannion. (*She drives the pin through the image in the approximate position of the heart, then straightens up, smiles grimly and replaces the image on the table*)
JANE (*coldly*) What are you doing?

(ELLEN *turns quickly to face the stairs, shielding the table from Jane.* JANE *comes down the stairs and moves up* L *of the chair* C. *All her movements are quick, lithe and feline.* ELLEN *turns with her and indicates the objects on the table*)

(*Contemptuously*) Witchcraft! There are better ways—surer ways—than that. Get rid of that stuff—(*she crosses to the dresser and takes her sewing-basket from the cupboard*) and go and heat the milk. See that there's plenty of sugar.

(ELLEN *picks up the objects and moves to the door down* L)

(*She turns, sewing-basket in hand*) You understand, don't you?

(ELLEN *nods and exits down* L. JANE *moves to the chair* C, *sits, gets out her work and sews. A door slams off* R. JANE *half raises her head, listens, then resumes her sewing.*

RICHARD *enters down the stairs. He is a very different man from the way he was depicted by Jane in the previous flash-back. He looks thoroughly ill, his shoulders are bent, his body shrunken, and his walk slow. He pauses at the newel post and looks at Jane. Whilst his voice is not very strong, it still has the veiled sneer*)

RICHARD. Sewing. Sewing. Always sewing.
JANE. Yes. Still your faithful Penelope, Richard.
RICHARD (*moving to* L *of Jane*) Ah, you remember me telling you that story, do you? (*He stands looking down at her*) You're a clever woman, Jane—an apt pupil—and a wonderful memory for the smallest detail. (*He crosses to the chair* RC) Penelope and her suitors, eh? At the time I was certain you'd never had a suitor. Now—(*he sits in the chair* RC) I'm not so sure.
JANE (*coldly*) What do you mean, Richard?
RICHARD. How I should laugh if ever I found out that you had.
JANE. Laugh?
RICHARD. At first. But—(*he slowly draws an imaginary strap through his hands*) afterwards . . .
JANE (*looking contemptuously at him*) Aren't you forgetting, Richard? You're old now—and sick.
RICHARD. But I'm still not afraid of any rival, my dear. Because I know you. You're like a cat. You never purr, but you see you get the best place on the hearthrug, the warmest spot by the fire. I'm the only one who can give you that.
JANE. You won't live for ever.
RICHARD. But when I die I'll arrange my affairs in such a way there'll be no inducement for anyone to marry you.
JANE. How's the novel going?
RICHARD (*rising*) Changing the subject, eh? (*He moves up* R *of the table* C) The novel's going splendidly. But I get tired, sitting at that desk. And the cramp—agonizing cramp—I can't go on sometimes for nearly an hour. But the book'll be finished well in time for the spring issues.
JANE (*picking up her scissors*) Then you'll be able to rest.
RICHARD (*moving above the chair* C *and running his hands over Jane's shoulders and upper arms*) Yes, and spare more time for you. I'm

afraid I've deserted you too much, in the evenings, lately. You must have been lonely.
　JANE (*dropping the scissors on the floor and bending to pick them up*) I read and sew.
　RICHARD. Of course. (*He turns towards the windows*) Howell not here yet?
　JANE (*startled*) Howell?
　RICHARD (*moving down* LC) I asked him to come up tonight.
　JANE (*relaxing*) Oh.
　RICHARD. I want to talk to him.
　JANE. What about?
　RICHARD (*crossing to the chair* RC) You'll know in good time, my dear.

　　(*There is a rap on the glass of the windows*)

(*He turns*) Ah, talk of the devil. (*Touchily*) Well, let him in.
　JANE (*rising and moving to the windows; resentfully*) All right. All right.

　　(RICHARD *sits in the chair* RC)

(*She calls*) Come in.

　　(JACK *enters by the windows. He is dressed, and looks as in the previous flash-back, except that his shirt is buttoned almost to the neck, but his manner is that of "Howell" not the "Jack" as pictured by Jane. At the moment he is nervous because of what he has heard. He stands just inside the windows*)

　JACK (*with a country accent*) Good evening, ma'am. Evening, sir.
　RICHARD. Come in, Howell, don't be nervous.

　　(JACK *moves down* C. JANE *moves a little down* L, *and apprehensively watches the others*)

I want to talk to you. I've had no time lately.
　JACK. What about, sir?
　RICHARD. Tomorrow we're going to start building the new room on the south-east corner.
　JACK. D'you think you're fit enough, sir?
　RICHARD. It'll do me good if I take it slowly. The bricks are here, and the mortar. I want you to see the plans. Go to that cupboard—(*he indicates the cupboard up* R) You'll find them there.

　　(JACK *moves to the cupboard, opens it and looks for the plans*)

(*He puts his hand to his throat*) My throat's like a lime kiln.
　JANE (*moving to the door down* L) I'll get your milk.

　　(RICHARD *leans his head against the back of the chair and closes his eyes*)

(*She opens the door and calls*) Ellen! Ellen!

(JACK *takes the rolled blueprint from the cupboard, and holding in it both hands, moves up* R *of* Richard. JANE *turns and sees him lifting the roll, preparatory to unrolling it. He senses her looking at him, and turns to her. For a moment the positions have a similarity with the moment in the first flash-back when Jack was lifting the scarf.*
ELLEN *enters down* L)

JACK (*unrolling the plan*) Here you are, sir.

(RICHARD *rouses, and takes the plan*)

JANE. Bring the master's milk, Ellen.

(ELLEN *exits down* L. JANE *moves to the chair* C, *sits and resumes sewing*)

RICHARD. Why do you have that woman about the place? I can't stand her.
JANE. She's very useful to me.
RICHARD. I packed her off once.
JANE. She'd nowhere else to go.

(ELLEN *enters down* L. *She carries a tray with a glass of milk*)

RICHARD. She must find somewhere else. (*He looks at the plan*) Now—let's see.

(ELLEN *moves to* L *of* JANE *and offers her the tray.* JANE, *with a movement of the head, indicates Ellen is to take it to Richard.* ELLEN *moves below the table* C *and stands by* RICHARD, *who is intent on the plan*)

JACK. Your milk, sir.
RICHARD (*looking up*) Oh. (*He takes the glass and sips the milk*)

(ELLEN *moves above the table* C)

I've just been telling your mistress, Ellen. You've got to go. Understand?

(ELLEN *stands looking stolidly at Richard*)

(*He looks at the plan and sips his milk*) I don't want to see you here in the morning.

(ELLEN *starts to turn away. Her look meets* JANE'S. JACK *notices this, and senses something, he does not know what*)

JANE. Get to bed now, Ellen.

(ELLEN *moves to the chest, puts the tray out of sight on it, lights a candle and goes up the stairs*)

RICHARD. I want you to mark out the foundations according to that. (*He hands the plan to Jack*) I shan't be able to do much digging, but I'll help with the marking out. Is it fairly clear?

(JACK *turns upstage slightly, so that the light from the lamp* R *shines more directly on the plan.* RICHARD *drinks his milk.* ELLEN *stands at the top of the stairs, the candle on a level with her face. She stairs evilly over the stair rail at Richard's back.* JACK *looks up from the plan and sees her*)

This milk is very sweet.

(*A twisted smile comes to* ELLEN'S *face, and she exits at the top of the stairs*)

JANE (*calmly*) It'll help you to sleep.
RICHARD. I'm not going to sleep yet. I'm going out for a walk. I need some fresh air.
JANE (*displeased*) You're not going far?
RICHARD (*rising and putting the glass on the table* C) Ten minutes, that's all, my dear, ten minutes. (*To Jack*) Well, d'you think we can work it?
JACK (*blurting it out*) I'm sorry, sir, you must count me out.

(JANE'S *needle pauses in mid-air. She does not look up*)

RICHARD (*becoming inimical at the thought of his plans being upset*) Why?
JACK. I—I . . .
RICHARD (*sharply*) Well?
JACK. I'm packing up—first thing tomorrow—moving on.

(JANE'S *hands fall to her lap, and she looks straight out in front of her*)

RICHARD (*bitingly*) So! I keep you here—five, six months—pay you for nothing in particular—and now, when I really want you —you calmly tell me you're packing up.
JACK (*reasonably*) I've stayed . . .
RICHARD. Just as long as it suited you.

(*Mechanically* JANE *begins to sew again*)

(*Cunningly*) What's happened? Why are you running away?
JACK (*uncomfortably*) I'm not . . .
RICHARD. Haven't I treated you well?
JACK. Yes.
RICHARD. Hasn't *Mrs* Mannion treated you well?
JACK. Yes.
RICHARD (*turning to Jane*) Better than many mistresses, eh, Jane?
JANE. I don't know about mistresses, Richard. But better than my masters have treated *me*.
RICHARD. One of your masters married you. (*He moves up* R *of the table* C) How have you done better than that—eh?
JANE. You're twisting my words.

RICHARD (*turning to look at Jack*) If I could be sure.
JACK. What are you driving at, sir?
RICHARD. You and—(*he turns towards Jane*) and ... (*He falters and his hand goes to his throat*)
JACK (*with a step towards Richard*) Something the matter, sir?
RICHARD. My throat—it's on fire.
JANE. Finish your milk, then.

(RICHARD *very quickly picks up the glass and drains it.* JACK *makes a slight movement as if to stop him, but is too late.* RICHARD *replaces the glass on the table, and moves to the chair* RC, *waving his hand feebly at the plan*)

RICHARD. Put that away—I can't do any more tonight. (*He sits in the chair* RC)

(JACK *moves to the cupboard up* R *and puts the plan in it*)

JANE (*putting her sewing in the basket*) You were saying if only you could be sure. What of?
RICHARD (*all the spirit gone out of him*) Nothing. Nothing. (*His hand goes to his throat, then he loosens his tie and undoes the collar button*)
JANE (*rising, picking up her sewing-basket and the glass and crossing to the dresser*) That's all you'll ever be sure of now, Richard—nothing. (*She puts the sewing-basket and the glass in the dresser cupboard*)
RICHARD (*rising and crossing towards the windows; feverishly*) I must get some air—some air.
JACK (*moving above the table* C) I'll come with you.
JANE (*half turning*) No!

(JACK *stops.* RICHARD *steadies himself on the table up* LC, *although there is no suggestion of collapse*)

JACK. But ...
JANE. Are you all right, Richard?
RICHARD (*moving to the windows*) Yes—yes. (*He turns and looks at Jack*) So, you're going, are you? Going in the morning. Then I shan't see you again, shall I.

(RICHARD *exits by the windows*)

JANE. Did you mean it?
JACK (*not looking at her*) What?
JANE. About going away.
JACK (*a little shamefacedly*) Yes.
JANE (*moving above the chair* RC; *all her pent-up emotion showing*) You can't.
JACK. I'm sorry, Jane, but ...
JANE. You're all I've got.
JACK (*moving down* C) I can't stay here. I'm sorry ...

JANE (*moving to* R *of Jack; urgently*) Wait, Jack, just a little while.
JACK. I . . .
JANE (*turning him towards her*) Only a little while—that's all I'm asking. He can't live long. He *won't* live long.
JACK (*more firmly*) I've made up my mind, Jane.
JANE. But you don't *know* . . .
JACK (*moving* LC) I know I've had enough.

(JANE *stands quite still. There is a slight pause*)

JANE (*her voice dead*) Of me?
JACK (*unwillingly*) Yes.
JANE. I see. (*She pauses*) What're you going to do?
JACK. Emigrate.
JANE (*emotionally*) No!
JACK (*turning to her*) I've behaved pretty badly, I know that—(*he moves towards her*) and this doesn't make it any better, but—oh, what's the use of talking about it. (*He moves towards the windows*) Good-bye, Jane.
JANE (*moving to Jack and holding on to him*) Come back.
JACK (*turning*) It's no . . .
JANE. You've *got* to come back—you've *got* to stay. It's gone too far. You belong to me and I belong to you, now—for ever.
JACK (*crossing down* RC; *with his back to her*) I belong to myself. I've always been free—I'm going to stay free.
JANE (*moving* C) Not any more, Jack, not any more. You see, I'm going to have a child.

(*There is a pause*)

JACK (*slowly turning to her; aghast*) A child!
JANE. Yours, Jack, yours.
JACK (*fiercely*) It isn't true.
JANE (*going to him and putting her hands on his chest*) It is.
JACK (*seizing her wrists and trying to force her away from him*) You tricked me into being your lover—now you're trying it again. Trying to trap me.
JANE (*trying to cling to him and slowly falling to her knees*) I'm the one that's trapped. If you leave me—I'm the one that's trapped.
JACK. What a damn fool I've been.
JANE. But it'll be all right, Jack. No-one'll know—no-one but Richard.
JACK. God!
JANE (*still clutching him*) And when Richard's dead . . .
JACK (*catching hold of her shoulders*) Shut up! Shut up! What sort of woman are you?
JANE. I love you.
JACK. You're bad—rotten—no good.
JANE. For God's sake don't leave me.

JACK. I'm leaving you all right.
JANE. Don't say that, Jack, please, please don't say that. Everything I've done's been done for you. Say it'll be all right. Say you love me.
JACK. Love you? I hate you. (*He throws her from him and turns away*)
JANE (*sobbing unrestrainedly*) No—no.
JACK (*turning to her*) I've finished with you.
JANE (*through her sobs*) What'll happen to me—what'll happen to me?
JACK. Good-bye, Jane.

(JACK *crosses and exits by the windows. The lights begin to fade*)

JANE (*clambering to her feet*) Oh, God, don't let him leave me. (*She sobs wildly*) Not after what I've done. (*She moves up* LC) What it's too late to undo. Jack! Come back! Come back!

(JANE *exits by the windows. The stage is now in darkness*)

(*Off*) Oh, God! I'm trapped—trapped—trapped—trapped—trapped . . .

(*In the* BLACK-OUT BENTLEY *enters down* L *and sits in the chair* LC. HOWELL *can be heard speaking*)

HOWELL. That was the last I saw of her. I went straight back to the tent, packed then and there——

(*In the* BLACK-OUT HOWELL *enters by the windows and moves below the table* C. *He is dressed in his chauffeur's uniform and holds the glass of beer. The lights come slowly up. The room is the same as it was before the flash-back*)

—and cleared out. Putting it plainly I'd got the wind up. I made for Southampton, avoiding the towns—not seeing any newspapers—got a job on a Union Castle boat—and jumped it at the Cape. Soon after I came to work for you. (*He puts his glass on the table* C) You know the rest.
BENTLEY (*ironically*) I know the *rest*—yes. (*Exasperatedly*) And that's all I damned well *do* know.
HOWELL. It's the truth, sir.
BENTLEY (*rising*) There *must* be something more—there *must*.
HOWELL. Why?
BENTLEY. Because it doesn't answer the question. (*He moves up* LC) If what you say is true—Richard Mannion was poisoned. There's no doubt of it. And there's no doubt Ellen was an accessory. (*He moves down* LC) But how did the body get two miles from here to that mineshaft?
HOWELL. Couldn't the two of them have carried it?
BENTLEY. No. (*He moves to* L *of the chair* LC) There must have been a third person. A man—a *strong* man.

HOWELL. But who?
BENTLEY. Why not you?
HOWELL (*thunderstruck*) Me, sir?
BENTLEY (*moving down* LC) You admit you were here that night. You'd already threatened Mannion . . .
HOWELL. What?
BENTLEY. Even gone so far as to try to kill him.
HOWELL. Where d'you get that from?
BENTLEY. Mrs Mannion.
HOWELL (*incredulously*) She said . . . ?
BENTLEY. In this very room last night—not knowing she'd ever see you again—(*he points up* R) she told me you hid in that cupboard and came out later intending to kill her husband.
HOWELL. But it just isn't true. Don't you believe me?
BENTLEY. D'you want to make me believe you?
HOWELL. Of course.
BENTLEY. Then tell your story to the police.
HOWELL (*startled*) The police!
BENTLEY. If you dare face them, knowing you've no proof—just your word—I'll believe you.
HOWELL. But . . .
BENTLEY (*moving up* L) We'll go along there now, shall we?
HOWELL (*moving down* R; *uncomfortably*) I'd rather not, sir.
BENTLEY (*forcefully*) But I'm trying to help you, Howell. If Mrs Mannion's accused, she'll tell the story she told me—she's no alternative. Don't you see the danger you're in?
HOWELL (*moving up* R; *doggedly*) I'm not going to the police.
BENTLEY. But in God's name why?
HOWELL. Because of the child.
BENTLEY (*after a slight pause*) You mean . . . ?
HOWELL. Vanessa. (*He moves up* R *of the table* C) She's not going through life knowing her mother's a murderess through any action of mine.
BENTLEY. You believe it's true, then—what her mother told you?
HOWELL. Yes. Vanessa's my child all right, sir—there's not a doubt of it. That's why I jumped at the chance to come down here—I *had* to find out. I'm sorry to upset your plans, but you must realize how I feel.
BENTLEY (*moving to Howell and putting a hand on his arm*) Yes, John, I realize how you feel. (*He crosses above Howell to* RC)
HOWELL. I deserted her before she was born—left her to live here, frightened and unhappy. I've *got* to make it up to her now. You do see that, sir?
BENTLEY. I see the further I go in this affair, the tighter my hands are being tied. I want to do my duty, and I come up against a mass of conflicting loyalties. (*He crosses above Howell to* LC) As a lawyer I should see that justice is done—as a father I

must show my daughter she's heading for disaster. But *she's* loyal to the man she loves, and to prove to her I'm right—that Mrs Mannion's guilty—I have to bring you into it. And because you have the same loyalty to your child as I have to mine—you refuse to help. (*He sits in the chair* LC) I just don't know what to do.

HOWELL (*moving below the table* C) Why not wait, sir, until after the inquest?

BENTLEY. It's a question of time.

HOWELL. Whatever happens it's going to be difficult to prove what you suspect.

BENTLEY (*rising*) What I *know*, John. (*He moves up* LC) After what you've told me, what we *both* know.

HOWELL (*moving to* L *of the chair* C) But if the medical evidence doesn't support us . . .

BENTLEY. It must.

HOWELL. But if it *doesn't* . . .

BENTLEY (*grimly*) Then Mrs Mannion is a very lucky woman.

(*The sound of a car arriving is heard off*)

HOWELL (*listening*) Is that their car?

BENTLEY (*looking out of the window*) Yes.

HOWELL (*moving towards the windows*) I'd better make myself scarce.

BENTLEY (*intercepting him*) No, John.

HOWELL. But . . .

BENTLEY. Stay here—meet her—face up to her.

HOWELL. I'd . . .

BENTLEY. She's accused you of murder, hasn't she?

HOWELL. Yes, but . . .

BENTLEY. Choose your weapons and fight her then. You may get something vital out of her.

HOWELL (*a little reluctantly*) All right, sir.

BENTLEY (*moving to the door down* L) I'll go out and keep David talking.

HOWELL. One thing, sir—I'd be glad if you'd tell me. Do you believe *I've* been speaking the truth, or . . . ?

BENTLEY. I believe you, John. But I still want to know how that body got into the mineshaft.

(BENTLEY *exits down* L. HOWELL *looks round for somewhere to conceal himself. He finds nowhere suitable, then suddenly thinks of the cupboard up* R. *He goes to it quickly, and hides in it. There is a short pause.*

JANE *enters by the windows. She wears outdoor things. She moves calmly to the table* C, *removes her gloves and puts them on the table, together with the shawl from her head. She goes to the mirror* L *and arranges her hair.* HOWELL *quietly comes from the cupboard.* JANE *turns quickly*)

Scene 2

JANE (*sharply*) What're you doing here? What d'you want?
HOWELL. To talk.
JANE. There's nothing to say.
HOWELL. Seems to me there's a great deal.
JANE. I'm not interested.
HOWELL. You will be. (*He moves up* R *of the table* C)

(JANE *turns quickly towards the windows as if to exit*)

And if you aren't, I dare say Mr Richmond *is*.
JANE (*stopping and turning*) What have you told him?
HOWELL. Afraid?
JANE. Haven't I cause to be? All I want is peace—forgetfulness. And just when they're in my reach . . .
HOWELL. I come back. Awkward, isn't it?
JANE (*moving* LC) But not as awkward for me as it may be for you, my friend. You don't realize that.
HOWELL. Oh, yes, I do.
JANE. Then . . .
HOWELL. Sit down.
JANE. I'm sorry, I'm . . . (*She takes a step towards the stairs*)
HOWELL (*more firmly*) Sit down.

(JANE *hesitates, then slowly sits very erect in the chair* C)

JANE. Well?
HOWELL (*moving down* R *of the table* C) What happened at the inquest?
JANE. It's adjourned till Friday.
HOWELL. Then should you and I be quarrelling at this stage?
JANE. What do you want?
HOWELL (*moving to the chair* LC; *musingly*) It seems I can make things difficult for you, and you can make them not so easy for me.
JANE. Go on.
HOWELL (*sitting in the chair* LC) So I would suggest—(*he leans forward*) that you and I—make a bargain.

JANE *looks at Howell under half-lowered lids as—*

the CURTAIN *falls*

Scene 2

SCENE—*The same. Evening, the following Friday.*

When the CURTAIN *rises,* VANESSA *is standing by the windows, gazing out.* ELLEN *enters quietly down the stairs, pauses, looks at Vanessa for a moment then moves to the dresser and unscrews the cap on the oil reservoir in the lamp.*

ELLEN. "The little birds sit in the nest on the tree——

(VANESSA *turns. She is rather keyed up*)

They waited till dawning,
But still ne'er came she."

(ELLEN *takes an improvised dipstick from her apron pocket and tests the oil level*)

VANESSA (*moving up* LC) Why d'you say that, Ellen?
ELLEN. It came into my head.
VANESSA (*moving up* C) You must have had some reason.
ELLEN. I'm old—very old. (*She chuckles*) I've no need to worry about reasons any more. (*She replaces the oil cap*)
VANESSA. Aren't *you* worried mother isn't back?
ELLEN (*shaking her head*) No more should you be.
VANESSA. But suppose—they've arrested her.
ELLEN (*moving up* L *of the chair* RC) You think your mother did it?
VANESSA (*uncertainly*) No—no, of course not. But so many people do. Mr Richmond—he must think so.

(ELLEN, *with an exclamation of dislike, crosses to the table up* LC)

(*She moves aside to make room for Ellen to pass*) Otherwise he'd have gone on staying here, instead of going to the pub in the village.
ELLEN. Maybe, maybe. (*She unscrews the cap on the lamp up* LC)
VANESSA. What will they do, Ellen, if the jury say father was—was—well, didn't die naturally?

(ELLEN *looks at her oily fingers and mutters*)

What will they do, Ellen?
ELLEN (*turning; to herself*) Where's that cloth?
VANESSA. Why don't you answer me?
ELLEN. I want a cloth.

(VANESSA *turns towards the cupboard up* R)

(*She turns and puts the dipstick into the reservoir*) Fuss and worry—fuss and worry. All about nothing. (*She looks at the dipstick*)

(JANE *enters by the windows. Her face is quite impassive. She wears her outdoor things*)

(*She peers up at Jane*) You got back then?
JANE. Didn't you expect me?

(ELLEN *chuckles and replaces the oil cap.* JANE *crosses to* LC)

VANESSA (*moving down* R *of the table* C) Hello, Mother.
JANE. Hello, Vanessa.

VANESSA. I didn't hear the car.
JANE. David's putting it away.
VANESSA. I—I . . . (*She runs quickly to Jane and hides her face on Jane's bosom*)
JANE (*putting her arm around Vanessa; gently*) What's the matter, child?
VANESSA. I'm sorry, I . . .
JANE. There's nothing to cry about. Everything'll be all right.
VANESSA (*looking up at her*) Is it—all over?
JANE (*sombrely*) Yes. Yes—it's all over.
VANESSA. What—was the verdict?
JANE. Suppose I told you it was murder?
VANESSA. No, no, it wasn't! (*She looks fearfully at Jane*) Was it?
JANE. So you still think it might be.

(VANESSA *hangs her head*)

And yet you cried when you saw I'd come back. Why, Vanessa?

(VANESSA *does not reply*)

Tell me.
VANESSA (*in a low voice*) I don't want anything to happen to you.
JANE. And that's all, isn't it? (*She passes* VANESSA *across to* L *of herself, moves below the table* C *to* R *of it, and removes her shawl. Harshly*) Well, at least *you* don't want anything to happen to me. But that jury did. They sat there—waiting—hoping—for evidence that would damn me. Just as Bentley Richmond, though he wasn't there—was waiting and hoping.
VANESSA. But what *was* the verdict?
JANE (*looking out front*) Accidental death.
VANESSA. Oh, thank God!
JANE (*moving to the chest and putting her shawl on it*) It *had* to be that. (*She takes off her coat and puts it on the chest*) That or an open verdict. I knew it—the coroner knew it. He gave them no chance to say anything else, once the analyst had given his evidence—had told them—(*she moves up* R *of the table* C) there wasn't a trace—not a *trace*—of any known poison.
VANESSA. Oh, Mother!
JANE. And that the fall *could* have caused the broken neck. (*She sits in the chair* C) At last, after all these years, justice has been done to me. I'd like to have them all here—all of them—those people who've pointed and whispered. I'd force them to their knees. And make them say they're sorry.
VANESSA (*kneeling beside Jane*) I'm sorry, Mother.
JANE (*more softly*) Yes, Vanessa, you doubted, too, didn't you? And David. David was so afraid the verdict would go against me he couldn't even wait for the inquest but had to rush off and marry that girl by special licence.

VANESSA. Soon they'll be gone for good.
JANE. Yes.

(VANESSA, *troubled, looks down*)

What's the matter, darling?
VANESSA. Nothing—only . . .
JANE. Surely, you can't have any doubts of me now?

(ELLEN *gives a low chuckle and mutters*)

(*She stiffens. Sharply, but not loudly*) Ellen! Go to the kitchen. Make me some coffee.

(ELLEN *picks up the lamp from the table up* LC *and shuffles out down* L).

Listen, darling, when David's gone, you and I will . . .

(DAVID, *full of high spirits, enters by the windows and stands up* LC)

DAVID. Well, Van, it's good news, isn't it?
VANESSA (*rising and moving to* R *of David*) Wonderful, David.
DAVID (*moving to* L *of Jane and putting his hand on her shoulder*) You all right, Mother?
JANE. Yes, David, quite all right, thank you.

(VANESSA, *slightly dejected, moves to the chest and stands with her back half turned*)

DAVID. And you're sure you don't *mind* Maureen and me going off tonight?
JANE. Of course not.
DAVID. We'll be back in ten days or so.
VANESSA (*turning*) Where is Maureen?
DAVID. Just putting a few things together. She'll be up here as soon as she's ready. Come on, Mother, say you wish us luck.
JANE. Of course I do, David.
DAVID. Good. (*He moves to the stairs and goes up*) I'll just dash upstairs and finish my packing, if you don't mind. I mustn't keep Maureen waiting.
VANESSA. You always did have the luck.
DAVID (*gaily*) Your turn'll come, Van.

(DAVID *exits up the stairs*)

JANE. Of course it will. (*She holds out her hand*) Come here, darling.

(VANESSA *moves and kneels* R *of Jane*)

When David and Maureen have gone, I shall have you all to myself. You don't know what that means to me. You don't know how much I'm looking forward to it. You see, darling, now all this dreadful trouble is over, we'll be able to have such lovely times together—I shall be able to give you all the things I never could in the past, and that's all I want, my darling, just . . .

VANESSA (*distressed*) No.

JANE. Why, what's the matter? Don't you *want* to stay with me?
VANESSA (*rising*) I want to get away, Mother—earn my own living, and be independent. (*She turns and moves to* R *of the table* C) And I'm sorry, but—(*she looks around the room*) I hate this house.

(*There is a rap on the pane of the open windows.*
HOWELL *is standing in the windows, peak cap in hand, and holding a white envelope*)

HOWELL. May I come in?
VANESSA (*pleased to see him*) Yes. Yes, please do.

(HOWELL *comes into the room and stands* LC)

JANE (*inimically*) What d'you want?
HOWELL. I've brought a note from the master, ma'am.
JANE (*holding out her hand*) What is it?

(HOWELL *hands the note to Jane*)

(*She reads the note*) So! Having got my son, whether he wanted him or not—he now wants my daughter as well, does he?
VANESSA. What d'you mean?
JANE (*reading*) "I've just heard the verdict, and am getting ready to leave for London. I will call on my way to say good-bye. It would give me great pleasure if you would allow me to take Vanessa for a week or so."
VANESSA (*delighted*) Oh, Mother!
JANE (*reading*) "I'm sure a change would be good for her."
VANESSA. Can I?
JANE (*crumpling the note*) No!
HOWELL ⎱ (*together*) ⎧ But . . .
VANESSA ⎰ ⎨ Mother—please. (*She kneels* R *of Jane, and*
⎩ *puts a hand on her knee*)

(HOWELL *watches them, annoyed and determined*)

JANE. Who does he think he is.
VANESSA. I'd love . . .
JANE. *He* won't take you from me.

(HOWELL *puts his cap on the table up* LC)

VANESSA. But it's only for a week or so. He says . . .
JANE. You're not going. D'you hear me? I won't *let* you go.
VANESSA (*rising and moving disconsolately* RC) I should have liked to see London.
HOWELL (*firmly*) Pack your things, Miss Vanessa.

(VANESSA *turns and looks hopefully at Howell*)

JANE (*whipping round in her chair*) How dare you!
HOWELL. Pack your things, miss. (*He looks at Jane*) I'd like to talk to you alone, ma'am.
JANE. Go to your room, Vanessa. Don't come down till I call you.

(VANESSA *goes up the stairs*)

HOWELL (*crossing to the foot of the stairs*) No need to take much.
VANESSA (*pausing a moment*) But . . .
HOWELL (*reassuringly*) It'll be all right.

(VANESSA *exits up the stairs.* JANE *rises and moves to* L *of the chair* RC. *She has temporarily lost her poise and is more the peasant. Her voice is low and full of hatred*)

JANE. Who d'you think you are, John Howell! Giving orders.
HOWELL (*moving above the table* C; *firmly*) I'm Vanessa's father.
JANE (*turning from him*) I'll deny it.
HOWELL. Deny it then. But you're not going back on our bargain.

(JANE *paces up* R)

I agreed to keep my mouth shut and you agreed to let me have Vanessa. Deny that.
JANE. Perhaps I did. But the inquest's over now. The whole situation's changed. (*She moves to* R *of Howell*) I'm going to keep Vanessa. She's mine—I love her.
HOWELL. A fine sort of love—keeping a child here, lonely—miserable.
JANE (*moving down* R) It'll be different now.
HOWELL. Different? You can't wipe out seventeen years just like that.
JANE. She'll soon forget.
HOWELL. She'll never forget. Not while she sees you every day—lives with you in this house.
JANE (*moving up* R) I'll take her away from here.
HOWELL. You can't.
JANE (*pausing up* R *then turning to him*) Why not?
HOWELL. Because you daren't.

(JANE *paces down* R)

(*He moves to* R *of the table* C) Give the girl a chance to be happy, Jane. Today's wiped out the years of suspicion—for the first time she's free—except for you. She's got to be free of you as well.
JANE (*starting to move up* R) She's . . .
HOWELL. Let Mr Richmond take her to South Africa.
JANE (*stopping dead; her back to the audience*) South Africa!
HOWELL. She can live . . .
JANE (*turning to him*) But I'd never *see* her again.
HOWELL (*agreeing*) No.
JANE. God! What d'you think I'm made of? Stone? That child's my life—d'you hear—my *life*. The one thing that's kept me going through all these miserable years—the one thing that's my *own*. What right have *you* got to her?

SCENE 2   TELL-TALE MURDER

HOWELL. A father's right.

JANE. She's *my* child, I tell you. I've given her everything— (*she turns from him*) and now *you* come and try to take her from me.

HOWELL. To give her what you won't—freedom.

JANE (*moving down* R; *contemptuously*) Freedom!

HOWELL. Freedom to live her own life.

JANE (*crossing to* LC) You're wasting your time, Jack Howell. Vanessa stays here with me.

HOWELL. Don't tempt Providence too far. Today you got away with murder . . .

JANE. How dare you say that!

HOWELL. But if I'd told 'em a thing or two . . .

JANE. What *could* you tell them? It's been proved today . . .

HOWELL. Nothing's been proved today. You poisoned your husband. I always suspected it—now I *know* it.

JANE (*moving up* L) Then why didn't the coroner know it?

HOWELL. Because the body in the mineshaft *wasn't Mannion's!* (*He pauses*) It couldn't have been.

(*There is a pause, then* JANE *laughs*)

JANE. Who thought that one up?

HOWELL. I did, and it's true, isn't it?

JANE. No.

HOWELL (*moving nearer to Jane*) You saw your chance when that body was found, and identified things that might have belonged to anyone.

JANE (*moving to* L *of him*) God, how I hate you!

HOWELL (*remorselessly*) What's your answer, Jane? D'you want the case reopened?

(*Very slowly the light begins to fade, as the sun sets*)

JANE (*crossing above Howell to* RC) I can stand it if I've got to.

HOWELL (*turning to her*) But you haven't got to. Let Vanessa go . . .

JANE (*moving to* R *of the chair* RC) No.

HOWELL. Then I must go to the police. Think what *that* means.

JANE (*sweeping below the table* C *to* LC) I don't care what it means.

HOWELL. The search'll start again. (*He moves down* R *of the table* C) And you know where it'll start. In this house.

(JANE *stops dead. There is a slight pause*)

(*He moves behind Jane*) You want security, don't you. Vanessa's the price. Not such a big one, either.

JANE (*moving down* C; *all the fight gone out of her*) All I have.

HOWELL. But how much longer will you have her? She wants to leave you, doesn't she?

JANE (*sitting slowly in the chair* C) Yes.
HOWELL. Then you'll let her go?
JANE (*almost inaudibly*) I haven't any choice.

(HOWELL, *satisfied, moves to the table up* LC *and picks up his cap. He turns as a thought occurs to him*)

HOWELL. Tell me—(*he moves down* LC) what *did* happen to Mannion's body?
JANE. How should *I* know? Richard Mannion's just—disappeared.

(*There is a pause.*
ELLEN *enters down* L)

ELLEN. Visitors. (*She stands to one side*)

(HOWELL *moves to the foot of the stairs.*
MAUREEN *enters down* L, *wearing a two-piece suit and carrying her handbag.*
BENTLEY *follows Maureen on. He carries his hat. He moves up* LC *and looks enquiringly at* HOWELL, *who nods*)

MAUREEN (*moving down* LC) We were very glad about the verdict, Mrs Mannion.
JANE. Thank you.

(ELLEN *exits down* L)

HOWELL. If you'll excuse me, I'll get Miss Vanessa's bag.

(HOWELL *exits up the stairs*)

BENTLEY. You're letting her come, then?
JANE. Yes.
MAUREEN. Oh, good. Where's David?
JANE. In his room, packing.
MAUREEN (*crossing to the stairs*) I'll go and give him a hand.

(MAUREEN *exits up the stairs*)

JANE. Won't you sit down, Mr Richmond?
BENTLEY. No, thank you.
JANE. I imagine we shan't be meeting again.
BENTLEY. No.
JANE. I hope you'll reconcile yourself to your daughter marrying my son.
BENTLEY (*moving down* LC) I must do my best.
JANE. You should be able to. After all, your "heredity" hasn't worked out quite as you thought. In spite of my mother's history, you were mistaken about me.
BENTLEY. I am *not* mistaken. I've tried to carry out what I consider my duty to my fellow-men. I've failed, and I'm ashamed of failing, because I haven't the courage to destroy my daughter's

faith and hope. *She* has beaten me, Mrs Mannion, not you. (*He moves to* L *of the chair* LC) I can only pray this marriage she made in secret will be a happy one.

JANE (*in a low voice; genuinely*) I pray that, too.

BENTLEY. But though the verdict this afternoon vindicated you in her eyes, and the eyes of the world, *I* am still not convinced of your innocence. (*He moves above the chair* LC *to* R *of it*) And if you *are* guilty, somehow—some*where*—retribution waits for you. You may have escaped justice, Mrs Mannion—you will not escape punishment. I can almost find it in my heart to pity you.

(JANE *raises her head. The tears roll down her cheeks*)

DAVID (*off; calling*) Ready, Van?
VANESSA (*off; calling*) Coming.
BENTLEY. I'll wait in the car.

(BENTLEY *exits quickly down* L. JANE *sits in the chair, elbows resting on the arms, her hands hanging loosely. Her whole body seems to have sagged. There is a pause.*

MAUREEN *and* DAVID *come down the stairs together, talking and laughing.* DAVID *carries a suitcase. They cross to* L *of* JANE, *who rises slowly, without looking at them*)

DAVID. Well, we're off, Mother. Going to give us your blessing?
JANE. I hope you'll be very happy, David.
DAVID. Thank you. (*To Maureen*) Shall I tell her, or will you?
MAUREEN. You, David.
DAVID. It's about this house, Mother. Maureen's persuaded me we needn't sell it, really.
MAUREEN. And we hope you'll stay on in it, if you want to.
JANE. It's very good of you.
MAUREEN (*gently*) Good-bye, Mrs Mannion. (*She moves to the door down* L)
DAVID. Good-bye, Mother. (*He moves to Maureen*)

(MAUREEN *and* DAVID *exit down* L.

VANESSA *enters quickly down the stairs. She is wearing a light coat.*

HOWELL *follows Vanessa down the stairs, carrying her suitcase. He pauses two or three steps from the bottom*)

VANESSA (*moving down* RC) Thank you for letting me go after all, Mother.
JANE. It's what you want, isn't it?
VANESSA. Yes. You won't be lonely, will you? It's only for about a week.

(JANE *shakes her head*)

(*She moves to Jane and puts up her face to be kissed*) Good-bye, Mo—— (*She breaks off*) Why, you've been crying.

JANE. It's nothing.
VANESSA. But . . .
JANE (*holding Vanessa's face cupped in her hand*) Let me look at you (*She stares at Vanessa's face as if memorizing it, then she once, gently strokes her cheek with the tips of her fingers. Then she puts her hand on Vanessa's shoulder, and passes her across towards the door down* L. *She is unable to keep her emotion from showing in her voice*) Now run along.

(VANESSA *crosses to the door down* L, *turns and looks at* JANE, *who stands with her back to Vanessa.*

VANESSA *exits down* L. HOWELL *crosses to the door down* L, *stops and turns*)

HOWELL. Good-bye, ma'am.

(JANE *neither moves nor answers.*

HOWELL *exits down* L. *The slight noise he makes shutting the door breaks* JANE'S *immobility. She turns slowly towards the door, then moves wearily to the windows and gazes out. The sounds of the cars departing are heard off. As if shutting out that part of her life,* JANE *closes the curtains. She stands holding the closed curtains, her head bowed. Only a glimmer of light is left in the centre of the room.*

ELLEN *enters down* L. *She carries a cup of coffee on a tray. She crosses to the table* C *and puts the tray on it.* JANE *turns lifelessly and watches her*)

ELLEN. So—they've gone.
JANE (*moving slowly and wearily down* L *of the chair* C) Yes—all gone.
ELLEN (*with her little chuckle*) Safe now.
JANE (*realizing the irony; hopelessly*) Safe! (*She almost laughs in her despair*)
ELLEN (*taking a short step forward*) Well—nobody's going to look for him now—buried in all that bricks and mortar. You can sell this house and get away from here.
JANE (*bitterly*) Don't be a fool. I can never leave this place. I've got to stay here for the rest of my life, Mother. (*She pauses then looks at the flagstones in front of her feet*) With him.

ELLEN'S *eyes follow* JANE'S. *They both stand looking at the flagstones as—*

the CURTAIN *falls*

FURNITURE AND PROPERTY PLOT

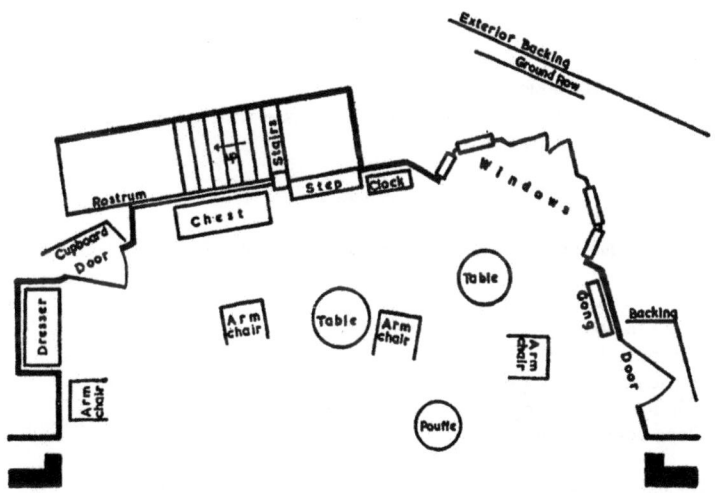

ACT I

SCENE 1

On stage: Dresser. *On it:* pewter and copper plates and mugs, ashtray
Chest. *On it:* brass or pewter candlesticks, oil-lamp, whisky glasses, bottle of whisky, decanter of sherry, soda syphon, ashtray
Table (up LC) *On it:* oil-lamp, ashtray
Table (C) *On it:* oil-lamp, sewing basket containing sewing materials and embroidery, fly swatter, book, box with cigarettes, ashtray
4 armchairs
Pouffe
Pair window curtains
Mirror (on wall L)
Pictures on walls
In cupboard up R: David's mackintosh, hat, duster, red silk scarf, long thin leather strap
Grandfather clock
Large gong
Persian rugs on floor

Lamp on table c, full up
Lamp on table up LC, half up
Lamp on chest, half up
French windows open
Window curtains open
Door down L closed

Off stage: Tray. *On it:* 4 sherry glasses

Personal: DAVID: sheet of paper with figures, matches
MAUREEN: handbag
BENTLEY: handkerchief, cigar case with cigars, cigar cutter, matches

SCENE 2

Set: On *table up* LC: tray. *On it:* pot of coffee, jug of milk, 2 clean coffee cups, saucers and spoons, bowl of sugar, 2 dirty cups, saucers and spoons
Replace pouffe to original position
Lamps full up
French windows open
Window curtains open
Door down L closed

Off stage: Heavy brass candlestick with lighted candle (JANE)
Cigar (BENTLEY)

ACT II

Strike: Coffee things
Dirty glasses
Maureen's handbag
Cigarette box
Ashtray from table c
Fly swatter
Battery table-lamp

Set: On *chest:* matches, clean glasses
On *table up* LC: matches
On *chair* RC: book
On *dresser:* mains table-lamp identical to battery lamp, matches
In *cupboard:* obviously different sewing-basket containing different piece of embroidery and sewing materials, scissors
Clean ashtrays
Transfer candlestick from dresser to chest
Lamps full up
French windows open
Window curtains open
Door down L closed

Off stage: Brass candlestick and candle (JANE)
Tray. *On it:* glass of milk (ELLEN)

Personal: BENTLEY: horn-rimmed spectacles
RICHARD: signet ring with plain seal
MAUREEN: handkerchief

ACT III

SCENE 1

Strike: Tray and milk glass, dirty whisky glasses

Set: *On chest:* candlestick, 2 clean whisky glasses
In cupboard up R*.:* rolled plan
Lamps out
French windows open
Window curtains open
Door down L closed

Off stage: Tray. *On it:* opened bottle of beer, glass (ELLEN)
Clay image, hatpin, withered hand (ELLEN)

Personal: HOWELL: handkerchief

SCENE 2

Strike: Empty milk glass
Beer bottle, glass and tray
Jane's gloves and shawl
Bentley's hat from cupboard
Lamps out
Disconnect lead of lamp up LC
French windows open
Window curtains open
Door down L closed

Off stage: Dipstick (ELLEN)
Suitcase (DAVID)
Suitcase (HOWELL)
Letter (HOWELL)
Tray. *On it:* cup of coffee (ELLEN)

Personal: BENTLEY: hat
MAUREEN: handbag

LIGHTING PLOT

Property fittings required: 1 battery oil-lamp
                                       3 mains oil-lamps
                                       Strip outside door
                                       Floods on backcloth
Interior. A living-room. The same scene throughout
         The MAIN ACTING AREAS are RC, C and LC

ACT I, SCENE 1. A September evening
     The APPARENT SOURCES OF LIGHT are large french windows up L, a battery oil-lamp C, a mains oil-lamp up LC and a mains oil-lamp up RC

To open: Sunset effect outside windows
                Strip outside door down L, on
                Lamp C, full up
                Lamp up RC, ½ up
                Lamp up LC, ½ up
                Effect—a pool of light C

Cue 1   JANE turns up lamp up RC   (Page 6)
            Bring up lamp to full
            Bring up lights covering RC

Cue 2   MAUREEN enters   (Page 8)
            Commence slow dim of lights as the sunlight fades. Reduce
                  lights covering area down L

Cue 3   JANE turns up lamp up LC   (Page 11)
            Bring up lamp to full
            Bring up lights covering LC

ACT I, SCENE 2. Night
To open: Moonlight effect outside windows
                Lamps full up
                Strip outside door down L, on

Cue 4   After rise of CURTAIN   (Page 18)
            Occasional distant flashes of summer lightning

ACT II. Night
To open: Moonlight effect outside windows
                Strip outside door down L, on
                Strike battery-lamp
                Set on dresser: mains oil-lamp identical to battery lamp
                Lamps full up

Cue 5   BENTLEY: "Very well"   (Page 40)
           Commence slow dim of all lights except for a spotlight focused
               on JANE's face, C

Cue 6	JANE: "Or the man I loved"	(Page 41)
	Commence fade of spot	
Cue 7	JANE: ".... make up my mind"	(Page 41)
	Quick dim of spot to BLACK-OUT	
Cue 8	ELLEN lights the lamp up LC	(Page 41)
	Bring up lamp LC *and lighting to cover area* LC	
	ELLEN lights the lamp R	(Page 41)
	Bring up lamp R *and lighting to cover area* R	
Cue 9	ELLEN blows out the candle	(Page 50)
	Quick dim of all lights to BLACK-OUT	
Cue 10	JANE: "Ellen!"	(Page 51)
	Bring lights slowly up	
	Bring in lamps	

ACT III, SCENE 1. Midday
To open:	Effect of sunlight	
	Lamps out	
	Strip outside door down L, on	
Cue 11	HOWELL: "... might have found out."	(Page 63)
	Dim all lights to BLACK-OUT	
Cue 12	ELLEN *mutters*	(Page 63)
	Bring up lights a little to cover area C *and* R	
	Bring up moonlight outside window	
	Bring in lamp R	
Cue 13	JACK exits	(Page 70)
	Dim all lights to BLACK-OUT	
Cue 14	HOWELL enters	(Page 70)
	Bring up lights as at the beginning of the Act	

ACT III, SCENE 2. Early evening
To open:	Effect of early evening sunshine	
	Strip outside door down L, on	
	Lamps out	
Cue 15	HOWELL: "... case reopened"	(Page 79)
	Commence slow dim of lights for sunset effect	
Cue 16	JANE closes the window curtains	(Page 82)
	Reduce lights except for a glimmer C	

www.ingramcontent.com/pod-product-compliance
Ingram Content Group UK Ltd.
Pitfield, Milton Keynes, MK11 3LW, UK
UKHW020016160325
456262UK00007B/561